COVER PICTURES:

FRONT: Crummock Water. Cumbria

BACK: Near Langholm, Scottish Borders

BONGO NIGHTS

A year's adventures in an ancient campervan

RICHARD HARRIS

© 2015 Richard Harris. All rights reserved.

*No part of this book may be reproduced,
stored in a retrieval system,
or transmitted by any means
without the permission of the author*

ISBN #: 978-1-326-49689-0

*Cover design, lay-out
and all photographs
by Richard Harris*

www.richardharrisnews.co.uk

www.bongonights.co.uk

Richard Harris
CA8 9JY
UK

'These people had not seen it at sunset,
they'd not known it in the dark,
they'd not witnessed the sunrise,
they'd not had it all to themselves
and they'd not sat on a rock
and sung songs to the stars'

– BONGO NIGHT 14
[MALIN HEAD, IRELAND]

PROLOGUE

IT WAS a pretty unlikely place for an adventure to start. But it was there – in a small unremarkable caravan site on a farm in a part of the country that's ignored by almost everyone apart from the people who live there – that one of the most memorable years of my life began.

Just a few miles up the road, in the majestic surroundings of the English Lake District, was a place where dreams are commonplace, where adventures being born seem just part of the landscape.

But where we were, taking an afternoon nap on a quiet caravan park because it was too wet to venture out, we were well away from any such excesses.

It was just another very enjoyable trip in our beloved Bongo campervan; a visit to an area

hose lack of specialness was the very reason we had chosen to go there; a brief break in a place we hardly knew existed until we looked at the map that morning.

Who would have guessed it was the beginning of something that would start out as a vague, crazy half-baked idea and develop into an obsession that would come to dominate my life?

Who would have guessed it was the prelude to a year in which I would end up going to places I'd never dreamed of going, doing things I'd never dreamed of doing and meeting people I'd never dreamed of meeting?

Who would have guessed it was the start of the wonderful, exciting, emotional and unpredictable adventure I came to know as my Bongo Nights?

I have owned a Bongo for six years now, ever since my wife Tricia surprised me by telling me she had been secretly saving up to buy me a campervan for my 60th birthday.

She told me to look on the internet to find the sort of van I'd like . . . and I came up with a Mazda Bongo, a small people carrier, imported from Japan and often converted, once here, into a fully-fledged campervan complete with a pull-out bed, a two-ring gas cooker, a sink with running water, cupboards, a wardobe and several fully working 13 amp sockets when hooked-up to the electrical supply in a caravan site.

"Brilliant!" she said. "That's the one I hoped you'd choose!"

The Bongo is a magical little vehicle – big enough to provide quite spacious accommodation for two people but small enough to go anywhere that a typical family car can go.

It has a roof known as an "auto free top", which lifts at the press of a button to create either more headroom for those inside or an extra compartment which is just about big enough for two more people to sleep "upstairs".

It is a vehicle much loved by its owners, and is fast becoming something of a cult, though it is often ridiculed by people who don't know it, and who think it somehow needs to be bigger, newer, flashier or more luxurious than it is.

Bongo owners have their own club, their own group on Facebook and their own special sign (raising one's hand above one's head in imitation of the elevating roof) which they are supposed to use when they meet one another on the road. Some people give theirs names – I've heard of Dorothy, Bernard, Buddie and Mrs Rusty, to mention just a few – but I've never been one for naming my cars so ours, and the one we had before it, is resolutely known simply as The Bongo.

Our first one was green, and we loved it dearly until some thief broke our hearts by stealing it from the streets of Edinburgh and taking it away to some grubby garage where, no doubt, it was dismantled and sold for spares.

Our second is white, with – thanks to a firm I found called Hippy Motors, who specialise in "funky car stickers for the free spirited" – lilac and pink dragonflies on the bonnet and a procession of small black hedgehogs on the back.

Despite the fact that the badge on the back proclaims it to be a Freda, it is universally known as a Bongo because in Japan Fredas (made by Ford) and Bongos (made by Mazda) are precisely the same thing and built in the same factory under different names. It has a 2.5 litre turbo diesel engine and can rattle along a motorway just as adequately as any other 17-year-old vehicle, and (though I'm not espousing any form of racing on the nation's highways) can outpace any of those idiots in their more boring cars who think it is somehow obligatory to overtake it purely on the basis that it is a campervan.

It is without doubt the most fun vehicle I have ever owned and the fact that it is not as smart, as big or as comfortable as some of the huge motorhomes we see on our roads these days only adds to its charm.

It is, in short, my pride and joy.

One of the joys of living where we do – in a small village in the north of Cumbria, a few miles from Carlisle and far enough from the Lake District to escape all the tourists who pack themselves shoulder to shoulder into such places as Keswick and Ambleside and Bowness-on-Windermere – is that nights away in the Bongo are easy.

A handful of miles north we have Scotland, with the wild mountains of the Border Country and the still largely undiscovered delights of the Galloway coast; to the east we have the glorious scenery upon which the Emperor Hadrian built his wall; to the west we have the Cumbrian coast, where the Irish Sea forms the backdrop to several very attractive seaside villages; and to the south we have the Lake District, still with some secret places known only to those of us who are lucky enough to live here and so have more time to explore than do the unfortunate crowds who have just the fortnight of their annual holidays.

Any one of those destinations would have been more than acceptable on Thursday July 3 2014, when Tricia and I decided to have a night away. But we'd been to them all before. This time we wanted somewhere new, somewhere different.

The map was fetched and a quick inspection told us there was one place to which we had indeed not been before. If we drove down the motorway, past the Lake District – or if we drove all the way through the Lake District and out the other side – we would come to an area unknown to either of us. An area of gentle countryside, not mountains; an area of estuary, not lake; and an area in which, unlike a few miles further north, tourists would be few and far between.

And so we booked ourselves into the Low Wood Farm Caravan

Park, near the village of Kirkby-in-Furness and ten miles north of the faded old shipbuilding town of Barrow-in-Furness (often described, disparagingly, as being at the end of the longest cul de sac in Britain).

Not far away were the honeypots of the Lake District, where tourists in their thousands visit every day to enjoy the splendour of some of Britain's most exciting countryside. They arrive there by bus, coach, car, motorbike and train – and on foot too, with their possessions crammed into huge packs which they lug everywhere on their backs. They walk, they climb, they cycle, they run, they swim and they jump off high mountains and fly across the sky on paragliders.

Thousands of them every day; millions of them every year.

And there, on that caravan park overlooking the Duddon Estuary, we had, it seemed, managed to avoid every one of them.

It was a quiet, peaceful, unexciting spot . . . but the adventure – though I did not know it at the time – had begun.

1
KIRKBY-IN-FURNESS
Cumbria
Thursday July 3

It was early in the afternoon and raining when we got to Low Wood Farm, so we pulled out the bed in the Bongo, climbed under a blanket (it was too hot for the duvet) and went to sleep.

When I eventually emerged from my slumbers I saw that there were a handful of other campervans and caravans there, but even though the worst of the weather had now passed over there was no sign of any humans attached to any of them.

And though eventually a man did appear from the van closest to ours, and I nodded to him in friendly fashion as I began the short walk to the little toilet block, by the time we roused ourselves to go for a stroll late in the afternoon we had still not spoken to anyone.

Tracey Edmondson, the owner, had told me that the village had a pub – the Burlington Arms – and that they served food if they felt like it but not if they didn't. Although I enjoy cooking and have come up with some pretty good one-pot dishes on the gas rings in the Bongo's kitchen, there never seems to be much point in going to such trouble if there is a cafe or pub serving food just down the road. So I followed Tracey's advice and phoned the pub to make sure that that night they did indeed feel like it.

We set off from the caravan site, down a path beside a field, across the main road and down the lane that led to the sea. Neither of us had any idea where that little road would lead us, but the village that unfolded before us at the bottom of the hill was not what either of us might have envisaged. With our preconceptions we were not expecting anything so charming and picturesque so close to Barrow! Lovely cottages; pretty, well kept gardens; steep banks of shrubs and flowers; and on the other side of the road, across a railway line, a huge open expanse of marsh and sand between us the sea.

We crossed the railway and followed a path along the shore, pausing for almost half an hour to sit on a tussock and enjoy the peaceful beauty of the place. It was there that the first germ of an idea came into my mind: What fun this was! How I'd like to do something like it more often! And why not? Now that I was retired (I had given up my job as a self employed freelance journalist just a couple of months before) what was to stop me? Every month? Every week? Yes, indeed, why not every week till the bad weather came? Or even – a daft idea! – every week throughout the year, no matter what?

The Bongo was made for such a thing, after all. Its "rock and roll" bed was good enough for two people, but even better for one; it had some, if not all, mod cons; it was warm and watertight; and it was small enough to go anywhere that an ordinary car could go.

As we made our way back into the village, up the steep hill to the pub (where someone was indeed waiting to cook our supper) the idea was beginning to take shape inside my head.

But I was briefly diverted by the conversation of the man behind the bar, who I I took to be the landlord. His accent gave him away as not being local and had the West Country burr of someone who had grown up, if not in Somerset as I had, then somewhere pretty close to it.

When I went to the bar for my second pint I was happy to hear him confirm he came from Keynsham, a small town to the east of Bristol once made famous by one of its residents, Horace Batchelor, who appeared on Radio Luxembourg several times a day to advertise his supposedly foolproof method of winning on the football pools. And our kinship didn't end there. He was a retired printer who had moved into the pub business after a career which had taken him, as mine had, to both Bristol and Nottingham, and he had known – or at least known of – many of the people with whom I had been associated early in my time as a journalist.

The next day, with the idea of my 52-week Bongo challenge still working its way around my head, we visited a place that I had wanted to visit ever since I first arrived in Cumbria 25 years before, but which was just a little bit too far away from home for a comfortable day out.

Conishead is an intriguing Gothic revival country house built on the site of a 12th century Augustinian Priory as a hospital for the area's "poor, decrepit, indigent and lepers". It has been a school, a hydropathic hotel (with a resident orchestra and its own branch railway line), a convalescent home for miners from the Durham coalfields and, in World War II, the biggest military hospital in the North-West of England, but for the past 45 years it has been a Manjushri Kadampa Tibetan Buddhist meditation centre – the sort of place that has always appealed to me, even though I have no special interest in religion in general or Buddhism in particular.

I loved it there. For an hour we wandered around its 70 acres of gardens and woodland that stretch right down to the sea, then we returned to spend another one sitting in silence in the Buddhist temple, an extraordinarily spiritual place, where I found myself quickly transported into a state of relaxation so deep and perfect that it surprised me. "It's a pity that that woman made such a commotion at the door," Tricia said as we left.

"Commotion? I heard no commotion."

It seemed that a woman had objected to being asked to take her shoes off as she entered the temple and had made her displeasure known both loudly and long, but in my state of deep meditation I had not heard a thing.

It made an interesting and worthwhile day . . . and proof that these Bongo Nights (yes, in my head I'd already started calling them that) could prove to add an intriguing and unexpected dimension to my retirement. By the time we drove away from Conishead I was set on my plan: I would spend at least one night in the Bongo for 52 consecutive weeks. Every few days from June to June, though summer, autumn, winter, spring and summer again, I would pack the van up and go off on my travels. Just because I could.

2
CARSETHORN
Near Dumfries
Friday July 11

Carsethorn is a tiny village in Scotland, on the shore of the Solway Firth, from where the mountains of the Lake District can be seen looming in the distance across the water. It has a few houses, a car park, a public toilet . . . and, in the Steamboat, a superb pub to which Tricia and I had been for lunch on a few occasions. The perfect place, I reckoned, to begin my year-long mission in earnest.

When I arrived there, on one of the most beautiful evenings of that almost entirely beautiful summer, I could see at once that the Steamboat was doing good business. Families were filling most of the tables in the beer garden which fronted the pebbly beach, and men were standing at the door, apparently trying to get through the crowds to the bar. The pub's own car park was full and the public car park alongside it had just one space left, which to my good fortune was overlooking the sea.

It was quite early (people in those parts seem to like to eat much earlier than I would normally choose) so I was in no rush. I politely pushed my way inside, bought a pint and escaped back to the beer garden to enjoy the evening sea air.

I found a vacant picnic table and sat down with my beer to wait for the hordes to finish their meals and go home.

When the licensee – a charming Polish lady whom I had met before on our earlier visits – arrived with two drinks for the middle aged couple at the next table I took my chance and asked her if she thought it would be all right if I parked the Bongo overnight in the public car park. I had no ulterior motive; I just wanted confirmation that it was not likely to attract the attention of any local vandals as I slept, but the man on the next table took matters into his own hands. "Why don't you move it into the pub car park later on?" he asked me. "We've got a campervan too and the chap behind the bar told us it would be OK, so I'm sure it will be for you too."

I thought I detected a flash of horror on the landlady's face. "But we do bed and breakfast," is all she said, but she said it in a rather hurt voice and it was clear she did not wholeheartedly agree with the barman suggesting that people could stay for free in her car park when they could much more profitably be shelling out £80 a night for a bed upstairs.

She knew she was in an impossible position though. She could hardly tell the couple that, no matter what the barman had said, they couldn't use her car park, and if she had to give albeit grudging permission to them, she could hardly refuse it for me. I tilted my head and smiled, in a wordless request and she, accepting she was beaten, graciously smiled back and said: "Yes, of course."

As soon as a space became available I moved the Bongo from its perfectly acceptable position in the public car park to an even better one in the pub's. I thanked the couple for their help and, while I tucked into my excellent meal of seafood casserole, learned that they were from Surrey, on their way to Glasgow, where they would be staying with their son, who, like one of mine, is a rock musician.

As darkness – and the cold – fell I went for a walk on the pebbly beach which despite its beauty and tranquillity always has an air of sadness, if not menace, about it because of what happened there hundreds of years ago.

In the late 1700s and early 1800s thousands of people left in ships from the little wooden pier there (there are still traces of it sticking out of the mud) as they fled destitution in Scotland for what they hoped would be better lives in America.

I always find it impossible to stand on the beach without imagining the despair of all those people, forced to leave their beloved homeland simply "to get more bread" as the ship-shaped memorial on the beach puts it – or, worse, of the convicts who were loaded onto ships for Australia after being herded down the road from the courthouse in Dumfries 15 miles away.

The next morning I awoke to find the high tide lapping just a few feet from the Bongo's front wheels. It was the perfect spot for a leisurely breakfast . . . if I had not been in the car park of a pub whose owners, I knew, would have preferred to be selling me a breakfast of their own. Diplomacy ruled, and I left Carsethorn without sending the glorious smell of cooking bacon from the Bongo through the pub's open windows.

Instead I drove a few miles up the coast to cook my breakfast at Glen Caple, a village where, I had been told, campervans were welcome to park overnight on a large car park next to the harbour.

It made sense for me to take a look, as I was passing on my way home, to see if it would make a good Bongo spot for some time in the future. It was immediately obvious that it would. The car park was well off the road, and it would be possible to park – as in Carsethorn – with the front wheels almost in the sea. There was a public toilet block (though whether it would be open all night I could not tell), a pub on the opposite side of the road, and a cafe serving bacon rolls for breakfast. And best of all, built into a small wall was a sign saying that overnight campervans were welcome, and it was up to their owners whether or not they put a small donation in the adjacent money box.

I had my bike on the back of the Bongo and was unclipping it for a short ride on the flat stretch of countryside along the coast to the Caerlaverock wildfowl reserve when a car came in and parked close to the harbour. I paid little attention until the driver got out and unloaded a handful of fishing rods and small boxes from the boot. Although he had his back to me, I recognised him instantly.

Here, miles from anywhere of any importance, in a sleepy Scottish seaside village that most people had never heard of, was His Honour Judge Paul Batty QC, Honorary Recorder of Carlisle, Cumbria's top criminal judge and a man who – after watching him for years as a freelance reporter at Carlisle Crown Court – I had the utmost respect and admiration for.

He turned and saw me.

"Richard!" he said, not surprisingly taken aback. "What are you doing here?"

Ignoring the fact that this was the first time he had called me by my first name (in the stately environs of the Crown Court it had always previously been Mr Harris or "the gentleman of the Press"), I explained why I was there.

"Well, you've chosen a good day – there's a bore coming this morning."

Having grown up in Somerset I knew about bores – especially the Severn Bore, which rolls up that estuary, causing a tidal wave big enough for people to surf upon – but I had never heard of one in the Solway.

He told me I would be able to witness the spectacle of the bore making its way past the harbour wall, as long as I was back from my bike ride within an hour. I returned in little more than 45 minutes.

"Sorry, you've missed it," the judge told me. "I made a bit of a miscalculation with the timing. But it wasn't a very good one anyway."

By now several other people – locals, ranging in age from some teenaged schoolboys on bikes to a couple of old men with a dog, all of whom seemed to know the judge as a regular visitor to their village – were also in easy conversation with him, discussing the prospects for a day's fishing.

"I don't suppose I'll catch much," he said. "The tide's wrong and the conditions aren't very good."

"Ha!" one of the boys muttered. "That's not why you won't catch anything. You won't catch anything because you're a crap fisherman."

I was still wondering how a teenaged boy could say such a disrespectful thing to Cumbria's most eminent legal brain, when I realised that both he, the judge and indeed everyone else in the group was laughing. And I wished that everyone who complains that our judges are out of touch could have been there to see it.

3
NEWLANDS HAUSE
Cumbria
Friday July 18

With the Lake District only just down the road from my home, I know there are numerous lay-bys, parking places, open fells and hidden valleys in which it is possible to imagine parking up for the night there.

One of the best of them is on Newlands Hause, at the far end of a valley which leads almost from Keswick (one of the Lake District's honeypot towns, where tourists go in their thousands to buy the boots and outdoor clothing which, I suspect, most of them will never use) and up into the wilderness lands deeper into the mountains above lesser known places like Buttermere and Loweswater.

After snaking for miles up the valley, through increasingly wild and spectacular scenery, the road suddenly reaches the top of the hill, before plunging down the other side, down an almost straight but breathtaking road to the village of Buttermere.

Right at the top there is a parking place – big enough for half a dozen cars – which looks out across a panorama that takes in Red Pike, High Stile and a bit of Great Gable.

It was there that I hoped to go for my third Bongo Night (and I knew of another almost equally good spot further down at Honister, on the far side of Buttermere, which would make a very good alternative if someone else had parked there by the time I arrived).

I stopped off in Keswick on the way, because Keswick, for all its busyness and brash commercialism, is a place which it is always fun to walk around.

The place was heaving with people. They dawdled on the pavements, they dawdled in the roads (the typical Keswick tourist has apparently grown up in some place where the motorcar has not yet been invented), they dawdled in front of shop windows and they dawdled in front of cafes which were closed and so would not be able to welcome them as customers for at least another 14 hours. I have seen Keswick a hundred times or more but I had never seen it so busy. In fact nowhere had I ever seen so many people with apparently nowhere to go.

At least, I thought, I would be able to nip into a pub and use the loo without any questions being asked because the bar staff would be far too busy to notice a man coming in off the street and heading for the gents without even ordering a pint.

I opened the door of the Dog and Gun – always one of Keswick's busiest pubs – and found, quite literally, three men and a dog. The landlord and two barmaids, who were leaning on the bar, looking bored, had nothing to do but watch me as I made a dive down the corridor opposite.

It was a similar situation in the fish and chip takeaway up the road, opposite the old Moot Hall in the town square. Staff there were always rushed off their feet, with customers queueing out of the door and into the street. But tonight it was empty and I was able just to walk in, get served and walk out in the space of just three minutes.

I sat on a bench in the square, eating my cod and chips and wondering what on earth was going on. I could not make up my mind. Was it a good sign that the town was so busy? Did it mean that all the people were in Keswick, so I would have Newlands Hause to myself as I hoped? Or did it mean that there were so many people in the Lake District that night that when I got to my chosen night-time parking spot there would be four campervans and three tents already there? There was only one way to find out . . .

When I got to Newlands Hause there was no one else in sight. It was exactly as I had hoped. The evening sunlight was bathing the panorama in front of me in a golden hue, the silver light was glinting on the small part of the waters of Buttermere that I could see, the buzzards were wheeling in the thermals overhead, the sheep were gently munching on the bracken and the only sound I could hear was of a small waterfall tumbling down onto the rocks.

And so it remained until another campervan – older even than mine – laboured up the hill behind me and pulled onto the gravel beside the Bongo. A young couple, hippies in another age, got out, stretched, smiled at me and unfolded an Ordnance Survey map against a boulder.

I did not really want to share my piece of heaven with them, but I realised it was big enough for both of us and I had no exclusive right to the place. And anyway they looked friendly enough, and they had no children or – much worse in my opinion – dogs to disturb the peace.

"Are you staying the night here?" I asked in what I hoped was friendly fashion. "There's plenty of room."

The man flicked his long hair out of his eyes and looked down at the map.

"No," we want to go a bit further yet. "We're hoping to find a pub and then to go on to somewhere nearby."

"You're in luck then," I said. "Buttermere, just down there, has got two pubs – or rather one pub and one hotel – and there are plenty of places for campervans in both directions.

"If you turn left there you'll come to Honister where there's a wonderful spot – nice and flat, well off the road and beside a river. That's where I was going to go if here had been full.

"And if you turn right instead of left at the bottom, the road will take you along the shore of Crummock Water, where there are several parking places, including one that's just about the size of your van, cut into the hillside so you can park very snugly in there with your bonnet facing the lake."

They thanked me nicely, got me to take a photograph of them with their backs to the view and drove off slowly down the hill. Apart from an elderly couple who parked briefly to exercise their two yapping dogs I didn't see another soul until next morning.

I got up early, as soon as it got light, because I wanted to get down to Buttermere before anyone else (it is a place which can quickly become full at that time of year on a sunny day). I parked the Bongo – the first vehicle in the National Trust car park – and decided it was so wonderfully peaceful I would go for a stroll before anyone else turned up. Which is how, astonishingly, I was walking around Buttermere (the lake, that is, not just the village) at 6.57am.

By the time I returned a few other cars had joined me in the car park, and the National Trust warden was setting out the stall of leaflets and membership application forms in the back of his Land-Rover. I wandered over for a chat, partly so I could tell him that I had not in fact spent all night in his car park (I suspected such a thing would be frowned upon) and partly because there were things I wanted to find out.

"What on earth was going on in Keswick last night?" I asked. "There were thousands of people milling about but all the pubs were empty. What was I missing?"

He grimaced and raised his eyes to the heavens (which was appropriate, as it turned out). He explained that we were halfway through the Keswick Convention, an annual meeting of evangelical Christians which brings almost 20,000 visitors to the town for three weeks in mid summer.

"There are thousands of them but they don't spend any money," he said. "They fill all the hotels and guesthouses and B&Bs so nobody else can get in, but they spend all day in their meetings and when they go out in the evening they just go for a walk.

"People like them don't go into the pubs, so the pubs and the restaurants are empty. There's a bit of ill feeling."

I went back to the Bongo and cooked myself a hearty, though somewhat delayed, breakfast of bacon, egg, mushrooms, tomatoes and fried bread. It was only afterwards that I realised the irony, that I had thoroughly enjoyed my time in Buttermere but – like the Christians in Keswick – had failed to put a penny into the local economy.

4
HAYDON BRIDGE
Northumberland
Wednesday July 23

Haydon Bridge is not the sort of village to which many people have ever paid very much attention . . . and they have paid even less since they stopped having to queue to get through it once its by-pass was opened five years ago.

It lies on – or just off, these days – the busy A69 road linking Carlisle with Newcastle, about 30 miles from my home, and, although parts of it are quite attractive where they overlook the River Tyne, it's not a place many visitors choose to spend very much time in.

But that's where I went for my fourth Bongo Night.

Our friend Trevor, who used to live next door to us until he had to move for financial reasons after his marriage fell apart, had moved to a flat there, above the Spar shop and his new girlfriend lived with her two teenaged daughters just around the corner.

It was a while since we had seen them so Tricia and I decided it would be a good idea to take the opportunity to combine that week's Bongo Night with an evening spent with our old friend.

Haydon Bridge has only one caravan park – Poplars, on the southern bank of the Tyne – so the choice was a simple one.

We arrived there on a sweltering afternoon, chose our pitch from a long line of empty spaces just a few yards from the river, spread a blanket on the grass . . . and fell asleep in the sunshine.

I awoke to a truly dreadful smell. Jumping to an obvious conclusion, I guessed that either the local sewage works had overflowed into the river or a pipe had fractured and was haemorrhaging something very unpleasant onto the grass alongside the campsite's toilet block. In my mind I was already working out how best to explain to the site owner that we were leaving and wanted our money back when Tricia told me she had found out what it was: It wasn't a lavatorial smell at all, but the pong of the vegetation on the riverbank rotting in the hot sunshine after being left exposed by the falling water level.

By the time Trevor arrived on foot in the late afternoon the temperature had dropped and the smell from the weed had eased to nothing more than a faint and only slightly offensive odour. We walked with him back to Diane's house, where she and her daughters were already busy with a barbecue. It was a happy evening . . . but all a bit surreal, knowing that at the end of it, though we could have been home in not much more than half an hour, we would be going back to a small campervan beside the river instead.

5
KENDAL
Cumbria
Friday August 1

I had long liked the idea of walking across Morecambe Bay, the huge expanse of sand that's exposed when the tide goes out.

It was pretty obvious I couldn't do it by myself – walking across such a place would be both daft and dangerous for anyone without much more knowledge and experience than I had – but once I heard that a man called Cedric Robinson was officially the Queen's Guide Across The Sands, and he took parties across for a small fee, I put it down on my list of things to get around to sometime.

I eventually got round to it in the summer of 2014. Of all my Bongo Nights it was the one that required the most planning – not least because two friends were coming on the walk with me, which meant we had to work out a plan involving two campervans, not just one. Camping in the wild was not an option (Tricia, who was coming with me to provide the shuttle service to take me to the start of the walk and from the end of it, doesn't share my enthusiasm for hopping over a hedge for toilet facilities; and nor did our friend Betty, who had a smart new VW camper, or Val, who would be staying in it with her). So after much scanning of maps and campsite guidebooks, the plan we set upon was this:

We would stay at the Caravan Club's Kendal site (which in fact is a few miles south of Kendal, nearer the start of the walk at Arnside). Early the next morning we would all leave for Arnside ten miles away in the Bongo, leaving Val's car and Betty's van in the site's car park. Three of us would then join the walk, with Tricia (who doesn't like walking on soft sand, so had no appetite for doing so across the whole bay) driving round to Grange-over-Sands where, in a few hours time, we would arrive on foot.

It was one of those occasions upon which I would have benefited from a little research.

In the months leading up to the walk I had formed an expectation in my mind – a picture of what it would be like walking across that huge expanse of sand.

I imagined setting off in the bright hot sunshine of summer, with maybe 20 like-minded souls, all reduced to almost tearful silence by the majesty of the landscape.

I saw us standing in the middle of the bay, gazing in awe at the Lake District mountains ahead of us and the Lancashire coast behind. I expected it to be one of the stand-out experiences of my life.

A little homework would have warned me that it would not be like that.

The weather was appalling, for a start (so wet and miserable that the closer we got to the walk the more I hoped it would be called off, if only on the grounds that the river we had to cross would be far too deep to be tackled in safety). The 20 or so walking companions I expected turned out to be more than 400 – a huge crowd which made it quite impossible to appreciate, let alone enjoy, the lonely splendour of the place. And although the Lake District mountains must have been there, they were hidden in the sort of drizzle that wipes out everything apart from what is happening immediately in front of your nose.I confess that as we gathered on the promenade at Arnside I could think of many other things that I would rather have been doing. We walked

along the coastal path, in a miserable procession of squelching trainers and dripping cagoules that confirmed all my worst fears. And when we branched out across the bay, standing wretchedly at the edge of the water before wading through it thigh-deep to the other side, I just wanted to turn back and admit the whole thing had been a terrible mistake.

And then . . . I began to enjoy it. It was all so absurd – the very idea of hundreds of people following without question as an old man led them across mile after mile of sand in pouring rain, and being happy to pay for the privilege – that by the time we reached the other side I was laughing.

I was happier still to find that Tricia had managed to find a parking space immediately next to the little railway station at Hest Bank where the walk ended. While most of my walking companions had to wait in their sodden clothes for the next train, in which they would cram together in a sweaty, steaming mass on the journey back to Arnside, I could simply climb abroad the Bongo, strip off my dripping clothes and change into new ones which were warm, dry and very welcome.

Afterwards someone asked me if I had enjoyed my day. I replied that I had indeed, but not in any way that I had been expecting.

6
MARSDEN MOOR
Yorkshire
Friday August 8

I have supported Bristol City through thick and (mostly) thin for 50 years – half a century of occasional flashes of excitement (we did, after all, once make it to the First Division, and held our place there for an astonishing four seasons, back in the days before the football world went mad and it became something called the Premier League) and long periods of failure, despair and thumping great defeats.

But here is nothing like the optimism felt by a football fan on the first day of the season. It is the one day on which all football fans can dare to hope, the day on which we can all dream that just for once the teams we love will do something to deserve our passion.

And so it was that I left home with a happy heart, heading for an overnight stop somewhere on the way to Bramall Lane, Sheffield, where Bristol City would be opening the season against the odds-on favourites for promotion, Sheffield United.

I had done some research (www.wildcamping.co.uk is an invaluable website which not only suggests places suitable for overnight campervan stops, but also even provides photographs of most of them to show what we can expect) and learned that the moors between Manchester and Sheffield would provide any number of potential resting places.

I settled on an enormous lay-by off the A635, high up on the hills above Holmfirth, the pretty little town where the long running TV series 'The Last of the Summer Wine' was filmed.

When I got there just as dusk was falling a couple of other cars were tucked into a corner of the lay-by, but I found myself a spot on the other side, facing the lights of the town which twinkled through the mist in the valley, pulled down the blinds, turned on the inside lights and settled down with a book until bedtime.

A couple of other cars arrived, stayed briefly (long enough for their occupants to admire the view, presumably) and went away, and by about 10pm I had the place to myself. Having thus satisfied myself that this would be a suitable place to stay the night, with neither vandals to disturb my slumbers nor jobsworths telling me I had no business to be parked there, I made the bed and changed into my pyjamas.

With a swooshing of gravel another car swept into the lay-by just as I settled down in bed, and arranged itself next to the Bongo, just a little too close for comfort, I thought. I heard opening doors, a man's muttering voice, and then a woman's, and pulled back the blind a little so I could see them standing on a boulder, arms around each other and looking down at Holmfirth.

I returned to my book, feeling a little uncomfortable that, when they had a whole car park to choose from, they had parked quite so close to me, but told myself that since I had chosen the best viewpoint I could hardly complain if they wanted the second best.

With another swooshing of gravel another car came in, and parked on the other side of the first, so that there were now three of us, parked side by side, all looking at the lights below us. A third joined us soon after, then a fourth, and I noticed that the drivers briefly flashed their lights in friendly greeting to the others.

Call me naïve, if you like, but I thought merely that a group of friends – knowing that my lay-by provided such splendid views of the dark hills with the lights of the pretty town beneath – had arranged to meet. Maybe one of them had the beer in the boot, I thought. And some sandwiches. Or some meat pies.

It was only when the cars kept coming, each accompanied by a flash of headlights, opening car doors, closing car doors, low muttering voices and giggles, that I realised the truth: Of all the lay-bys in that part of Yorkshire I had chosen the one favoured by the members of the Greater Manchester dogging community (and for readers even more naïve than I, I should explain that "dogging" is the meeting in lay-bys of people wanting sex in cars with strangers).

I had not been threatened, laughed at or inconvenienced in any way (and, in case you're wondering, nor had I been invited to join in, even though I was presumably the only one lucky enough to boast a double bed), but my lay-by suddenly seemed less perfect than it had when I had arrived. I was, I confess, embarrassed to be there, and anyway it's quite difficult to get to sleep knowing that the man in the Ford Orion just a few feet away is busy having enthusiastic sex with the woman who's just stepped out of the VW Golf.

I put my shoes on, climbed over into the driver's seat and started the engine.

I should explain that when sleeping anywhere other than in an official camping site, I always lock all the doors, leave the key in the ignition and try to keep enough space around me so I can drive out forwards and escape in case of emergency.

So it was that in that lay-by above Holmfirth I had parked the Bongo not with its bonnet snugly against the low perimeter wall, but about six feet back from it and with the front wheels already pointing sharply to the right.

I revved the engine, turned on the headlights (hoping that nobody would take that as a sign that I wanted to join in their games) and swung the Bongo round in a sharp turn.

As I turned towards the exit another car swooped in, flashing its headlights as if to celebrate its arrival and blinding me so badly that I nearly crashed into a grassy bank which, though it ran across the middle of the lay-by for almost all its length, I had somehow failed to notice before. I skidded to a halt just a few inches from a small tree and, with embarrassment piled upon embarrassment, slung the Bongo into reverse, in order to complete the three-point turn necessary for me to make my escape. I looked at my watch. It was 2am. A fine time to be driving – half asleep and in my pyjamas – across wild moorland looking for a camping place . . .

I eventually remembered that wildcamping.co.uk had suggested a smaller lay-by a few miles north of Holmfirth, on a narrow country road in a place even more remote than the one I had just left. It took some finding but, after an hour's increasingly desperate driving. find it I did and – in the dark – judged it to be more than adequate.

It was the sun that woke me. And when I peered out beneath the blinds I could see that the place in which I had ended up was indeed remote. Wild moorland in front of me, behind me and to my left . . . and to my right more moorland falling away steeply into a deep valley on the other side of a fence.

I got out of the Bongo to admire the view. Then I saw . . . The fence had faded bunches of flowers tied to it, and a teddy bear and some handwritten notes. Obviously a memorial to some poor soul who had died on the road there, I assumed. It was a strange place for any unfortunate driver to have met his death, I thought, because the road was nowhere near wide or straight enough for any vehicle to get up to anything like a lethal speed.

And then I saw there was photograph attached to a fence post. And the face in the picture was unmistakable.

Keith Bennett was 12 years old when he went missing in 1964. Today he is the only one of the Moors murder victims – five children killed by Ian Brady and Myra Hindley between July 1963 and October 1965 – whose body has never been found. I had spent the night near the place where his family believe he must lie.

In the circumstances it hardly seems appropriate to dwell too long on all that happened on the rest of the trip. I'll just say that Bristol City defied all the predictions and beat Sheffield United 2-1, beginning a 13-game unbeaten run (longer than any other team in the football league) and, after many years of gloom and disappointment, putting a smile back on the faces of their long-suffering supporters.

7
DERWENTWATER
Cumbria
Monday August 11

Derwentwater is not (quite) the most beautiful lake in the Lake District – for my money that accolade goes to Ullswater, which just happens to be the closest one to where I live – but it does have one great advantage over most of the rest: There's a superb walk all the way around it.

So when a friend who had just bought a campervan (a VW rather than a Bongo, but I suppose she can't have everything) told me that the National Trust allowed members to spend the night in their car parks along the eastern shore of Derwentwater, it left me with an easy decision to make about where to go next.

She told me that she had taken her van – which she had named Tallulah – to the lake, just for an afternoon out, and she had got into conversation with the chap trying to sell National Trust memberships at Kettlewell, a car park particularly popular among people with canoes and kayaks to launch from its gentle pebble beach. He had seen her van and told her – even before she had had a chance to ask – that although overnight parking was not officially allowed there the Trust turned a blind eye to it if the vehicles had membership badges on their windscreens.

As a long standing member of the National Trust I needed no further invitation! So I arrived at Kettlewell late in the afternoon, determined – despite the intermittent rain – to set off from there to walk around the lake, stopping off two-thirds of the way round in the Dog and Gun pub in Keswick, an establishment where the range and quality of the local beers on offer is matched only by their superb goulash (large or small, meaty or vegetarian, with dumplings).

I'm not a particularly enthusiastic fell-walker – the fact that I've done nearly half the 214 Wainwrights (the Cumbrian fells that Alfred Wainwright, the doyen of fellwalkers listed as being worth climbing) owes more to happenstance than any wish to get them all ticked off as many people do. But a ten-mile walk around a lovely lake on a summer's afternoon is something to be savoured. Especially when it includes a visit to one of my favourite pubs.

I walked fast, as I always do, and my spirits were not dampened even by the frequent showers which saw me putting on and taking off my cagoule so often that in the end I thought "Oh sod it!" and simply left it off and got wet. As I reached Portinscale, a large village which has a couple of pubs and a lay-by much favoured by owners of motorhomes, the showers ended – but only so they could be replaced by the sort of downpour that leaves the unsuspecting drains and gutters unable to cope.

This time I put on my cagoule and kept it on. Yet as suddenly as it had started, the rain stopped. The sun came out, and I was able to take off my cagoule in time to hope I would then dry out sufficiently (the cagoule had leaked in several places, and anyway it was too short to have offered any sort of protection to my legs) by the time I had completed the couple of miles to Keswick. When I walked into the Dog and Gun I was quite literally steaming. My hair was still plastered to my head. My trousers, soaked from mid-thigh to ankle, were clinging to my legs, and my walking boots squelched whenever I moved my feet on the flagstone floor.

And – unlike the last time I had been in the place, on Bongo Night No 3, when the bar staff outnumbered the customers – the pub was heaving. As I approached the bar the landlord was busy turning away a family of four, telling them they had no hope of getting a table within the foreseeable future so they might be best advised to go somewhere else. I had no intention of going anywhere else (my heart was set on a goulash, for one thing) so I gave the landlord a damp grin and told him I'd have a pint and would then be happy to wait for as long as it took to find somewhere to sit.

In most pubs the bar staff would simply have told me I was welcome to stand by the bar until a table became available, but I'd have to find that table myself, but here the landlord was going out of his way – literally – to make me welcome. He told me there might be no need to wait and established me on a table occupied by a middle aged couple who welcomed me with sympathetic smiles and told me they would not mind at all if I tucked into a goulash (large) in front of them while they were genteely sipping their lemonade and limes.

The goulash was as delicious as I knew it would be, and I scoffed it, probably far too quickly, while finding out as much as I could about my two table-mates. She was a Yorkshire lass, she told me (unnecessarily, since her accent betrayed as much), but she now lived in Alsace, where not long before she had married a Frenchman, on whose behalf she apologised for the fact that he could not join in our conversation since he could neither speak nor understand a word of English. I was flattered that she found some of my conversation interesting enough to translate to her husband – and pleased when his eyes widened in surprise when she passed on the news that I was spending the night in a campervan and would be doing something similar for one night a week for the next year or so. To a Frenchman, it seemed, that was a pretty crazy thing to do.

They waited until I'd finished my goulash, then excused themselves because they had to go back to their guesthouse for supper.

"I bet it won't be as good as that," I said, nodding towards my empty plate, but the Yorkshire lady looked unconvinced, while her husband merely smiled as he thought he should.

With a table to myself I was now in something of a predicament. I wanted – no, needed – another pint, but I knew that if I went to the bar I would be in danger of losing my seat, because the pub was still full of people looking around desperately for somewhere to sit.

I caught the eye of one of them, a young man leaning on the bar, who, like his girlfriend, was making short work of a pint of local Landlord ale. He leaned forward to hear what I was obviously about to say to him.

"You're very welcome to sit here at this table," I told him. "As long as you don't mind me coming back and sharing it with you when I've got another pint."

It never entered my head that, though they were obviously foreign, they might not understand what I was saying. And the speed at which they left their places at the bar and joined me at my table told me they understood very well . . . and did not mind at all.

I'm pretty quick at deciding if I like people (too quick, probably, because I often find myself disliking people on first impressions, only to have to revise my opinion later on when I've got to know them better). And these two I liked immediately.

I soon discovered that his name was Pascal and hers was Julia, and that they were one half of a folk-rock band called Postcard from Beirut, who – though the other two members had gone straight home after playing at a music festival in Oxford – had chosen to take the scenic route back to Lebanon and ended up in Cumbria.

"It's because we're a couple," Julia told me, as if that explained everything.

I told them about my son Will and his band which is not much different from theirs; about how I'd just bought a new guitar because after playing a couple of songs at my 65th birthday party I'd discovered I wasn't as bad as I thought ("You're never too old to be a rock star," Julia assured me); and swapped details of websites where examples of our various music could be found.

Pascal told me he had a love of English beer – something he demonstrated by the speed at which he drank it – and that they had spent part of the day on a tour of Keswick brewery (an establishment that I, a near-local, did not even know existed).

And Julia told me how much they loved the Lake District, despite the rain, and how lucky they were to have ended up by chance in Keswick on their circuitous journey home to the Middle East.

But they reserved their greatest enthusiasm for what they called my "Great Adventure", when I told them of my plan for 52 Bongo Nights.

"That's a great idea," said Julia. "You must do it!"

Pascal had no doubt that I would. "You will enjoy it so much that when you've finished you will have to do it again – but next time you will be doing it for two nights a week," he said. "And the next year for three nights a week. And . . ."

I stayed with Pascal and Julia in the pub until the time came when I knew I would have to leave if I was to get back to Kettlewell and the Bongo before it got dark. As I left Pascal called after me "If you're ever passing Beirut please call in and see us".

As I walked back along the shore of Derwentwater – a beautiful walk even in the half light – I told myself that my Bongo Nights were going rather well. And meeting some very lovely people was turning out to be a bonus I had not expected.

Back at the car park I found that I had it to myself . . . apart from a big old fashioned campervan which, closer inspection showed, was in fact more of a works van which had two canoes on the top and not much more than a couple of mattresses and a camping cooker inside. It was home to a couple from Lancashire and their nine-year-old son.

Over the camp fire that they had built on the beach to keep the midges away, they told me they had been there for three days, and that the National Trust warden was well aware of it and had not voiced one word of complaint.

I moved the Bongo closer to the lake so I'd be able to look out of the window and see the view when I woke up, and settled down to a night's sleep that I knew would be a good one. No doggers. No boy racers. No wondering if some jobsworth would wake me up in the night to tell me I should not be there. Just the sound of the water lapping gently over the pebbles in the wind.

I was brought heavily back down to earth – almost literally – the next morning. I was tidying up the Bongo after breakfast when I stood up in the back and leaned over the front seats to raise the electric blinds with the switches on the dashboard. Then, without looking or even thinking, I went to sit down on the bed which I knew was behind me. Except it wasn't. I had forgotten that I had already stowed the bed away. So instead of sitting on the soft mattress, made even softer by a thick duvet, I fell to the floor, smashing my back against the unforgiving metal and wood frame of the bed. It was like having a 16-stone hammer blow to my back.

I sat on the floor for several minutes, folded up in a Z-shape between the front seats and the stashed-away bed, gasping for breath and totally unable to move. I knew the only people likely to hear me if I called for help were the couple and their young son in the van at the other end of the car park, and there was no sign that they were awake yet.

I reckoned that I had two choices – stay where I was until the day trippers began to arrive, in the hope that one of them might come close enough to hear my cries, or somehow extricate myself . . . no matter how painful it might be. I chose the latter. I slowly rolled onto my side and, after grabbing the top of the cupboards alongside me, dragged myself to my knees. I was still on my knees when I got out of the van, and still doubled up as I slowly stumbled around the outside of it and, gasping from the pain, slumped into the driver's seat.

I needed to warn Tricia, but didn't want to alarm her, so sent her a text: "On my way. Could do with hot bath cos I've bashed my back. I'm OK but will have a bruise! See you soon."

That afternoon my doctor told me to lift my shirt. "Christ! That's going to bloody hurt!" he said (stating the obvious, I thought). He established that I had probably not done myself any lasting damage. I had somehow managed to twist my body immediately before the impact, so the blow caught me slightly to the side, in the space between my hip bone and my ribs, rather than directly across my spine, so with luck I had suffered nothing worse than a very painful soft tissue injury.

He prescribed me codeine for the pain, told me to go back to him if I noticed I was peeing blood (that would have been a sign of a damaged kidney) . . . and wished me luck in what he described as my "noble ambition" to spend 52 nights Bongoing.

He was right. It did bloody hurt. I yelped in pain for more than a fortnight, whenever I moved or put unwelcome pressure on my back, and even something as simple as getting into bed was a manoeuvre I could achieve only by doing a gentle belly flop onto the mattress. And that was not all. It soon became clear that either the blow itself or the painkillers I was prescribed to deal with it caused me what I shall delicately call an "upset stomach" for six months. And it was even longer than that before my back stopped hurting.

8
CULROSS
Fife
Friday August 29

A Bongo trip with our two grandchildren has become something of an annual event. It was something we decided to do as soon as Abigail was old enough, so when she was five we took her to Stonehaven (a seaside town only 25 miles or so from her home, and so a place she knows very well) where there was an excellent caravan park, owned by the local council, just across the road from the beach.

What we had not expected on that first trip was that Abigail's little brother Elliott, who was just two, would be coming with us too.

But when we arrived at our son's house to collect her, and saw an excited Elliott standing beside her, clutching his bulging rucsac with Winnie The Pooh poking out of the top, it was pretty obvious we were wrong in thinking he was too young for such an adventure.

That night in Stonehaven was so successful we did another one the following year – to another seaside campsite, at Banff on the north-facing coast near Peterhead, and in 2014, the year of my Bongo Nights, we did another one, this time back in Stonehaven, where our old campsite had been bought and "improved" at great expense by the Caravan Club.

On the way we had time to spend a night at a small caravan park near the glorious little town of Culross – or the Royal Burgh of Culross, to give it its full title. Culross, which stands on the northern shore of the Firth of Forth, is a delightful place, and not without cause does it call itself as "a town that time has passed by".

The tourist board describes it as "an almost perfect example of a Scottish burgh of the 17th and 18th centuries" and its buildings – many of them protected by the National Trust for Scotland – still boast the wonderful pantile roofs and crows' feet gables they were built with more than 400 years ago.

It was there that Tricia and I chose to stop off on our way north, in a Caravan Club Certificated Location (CL) down a very long and bumpy track on farm a couple of miles from the town.

CLs are Caravan Club sites which cater for a maximum of five campervans or caravans, without any of the unnecessary facilities – shop, bar, games room, TV lounge and so on – found at the bigger sites. Some have a toilet block and showers, some have electric hook-ups, and some have neatly laid-out pitches with hard-standing for the van; others have no facilities at all, and are simply fields from which a farmer is trying to make a little extra money.

The one at Culross was towards the bottom-end of the scale. In a field a short walk from the farm (in whose outbuildings was found the single, rather ill-kept toilet), it boasted a cold water tap and absolutely nothing else.

The track down which we had arrived continued towards the sea, so once it stopped raining (we had parked the Bongo beside a hedge, and true to form pulled out the bed and went to sleep while the bad weather passed) we walked down it until we found ourselves on the outskirts of the town.

Culross, with its winding cobbled streets and seductive nooks and crannies, is a place that demands to be wandered around and explored on foot, so that's what we did until Tricia found herself needing a loo.

We ventured into the pub, the Red Lion, where we encountered the best barmaid I have ever had the pleasure of being served by. She was smiling, welcoming and efficient, and – though she told us she did not drink the stuff herself – could describe in some detail every one of the beers available from the hand pumps on the bar.

We had planned only to have a drink (and use the toilet) and to go back to the Bongo for some sort of quick pasta supper, but once we smelled the deliciousness of the odours coming from the kitchen we decided that we would have a pub meal instead.

It was too early for my taste, though, so we booked our table for seven o'clock – an hour later – and walked for half an hour along the coastal path in the sunshine beside the sea. After precisely 30 minutes we turned around and walked back to the pub, arriving at the bar, with great satisfaction, at exactly 7pm.

Our meal was excellent (much better than anything I could have conjured up in the Bongo) but even better was the sight of the barmaid doing the job she did so well. She pulled pints, served food, cleared tables, chatted with customers, tidied up, closed doors that had accidentally been left open, opened those that had accidentally been closed . . . and never stopped smiling.

Some people are born to be musicians, painters, doctors or nuclear scientists; this lady was born to work in a pub. "If I owned a pub I would want her to come and work for me," I told Tricia.

At the end of the evening, as we left, Tricia thanked her and passed on what I had said.

For the first time in the evening the young woman seemed to be a bit flustered.

"That's the nicest thing anyone has ever said to me," she said.

9
STONEHAVEN
Aberdeenshire
Saturday August 30

With two excited grandchildren we arrived at the Stonehaven caravan site between showers. It had clearly changed since our visit two years before – and, from our point of view, not for the better.

It's true that the site was perfectly tidy, pitches were all big and beautifully laid out, and the toilet block (complete with showers, laundry and drying room) was immaculately kept and sparkling.

Our problem was that we needed to use our awning – a tent that clamps to the side of the Bongo, providing the extra living accommodation in which Tricia and I would sleep while the children used the bed in the van. Under Caravan Club rules, vans – whether campervans or caravans – had to park precisely in the middle of the gravelled pitches. Which is fine for vans much bigger than ours, as most Caravan Club members' are. But thanks to the "improvements" the pitches were now so big that for small vans like ours, which came nowhere near filling the pitches, any awning would also have to be on the gravel, rather than on the grass, which is where we had been able to erect it on our last visit.

The obvious solution would have been to park the Bongo off-centre, to the side of the pitch, so that while the van itself would be on the gravel the awning attached to it could be on the adjacent grass.

The wardens explained that under "fire regulations" this was not possible. They were very understanding as I explained that, since the Bongo was not really big enough for two adults and two children, we had something of a problem: An awning set on gravel would be worse than no awning at all – apart from the fact that the sharp stones would almost certainly puncture the built-in groundsheet, it would be impossible to sleep, let alone sit, read stories, play games or just enjoy being with our two grandchildren on gravel.

The wardens, bound as they were by Caravan Club regulations, seemed to have no answer, until suddenly one of them exclaimed: "Cardboard!". And so it was that for the next 20 minutes two small children were seen lugging great boxes and sheets of cardboard across the Stonehaven caravan park, from the rubbish compound to the Bongo, so we could put a relatively soft and smooth insulating base between the gravel and the groundsheet.

It was not a perfect solution, but it was good enough and at least it spared us having to disappoint the children by looking at the last minute for a grassy campsite in a less ideal location.

For Stonehaven is indeed an ideal location for a couple to take their grandchildren. It has all that is needed for a happy mini holiday with children of that age – a huge playground within walking distance, a beach, an award-winning fish and chip shop and, in Auntie Betty's, a wonderful ice cream emporium that sells the stuff in undreamed-of quantities and variations.

Our presence was not welcomed by all, however. As we were packing up the Bongo the next morning I fell into conversation with our neighbour, the owner of a huge caravan towed behind an almost equally large black 4x4. Either of those two vehicles looked as though it could have eaten the Bongo for breakfast, and I made some such such comment to the man, before explaining the problem with the gravel and why there were still sheets of cardboard lying around, which we had not yet had time to clear away. To say he was not sympathetic is putting it mildly.

He made it very clear that in his eyes a newly-improved Caravan Club site was not the place for a Bongo. "Well, it is the *Caravan Club*," he muttered, before turning his back on me and walking away, scuffing up the gravel as he went.

10
STONETHWAITE
Cumbria
Saturday September 6

Among the people taking the most avid interest in my Bongo adventures were my friend Alison and her then partner Damien, who had an ancient VW campervan – even older than my Bongo – in which they frequently camped in Cumbria and on the North East coast.

For my tenth Bongo Night Alison suggested taking both vans and camping together in a small site run by the National Trust at Stonethwaite, a tiny village at the far end of the Borrowdale valley in the Lake District.

Damien (an excellent guitarist) and I (not so) would take our guitars and we would have a happy evening singing songs and chatting, eating and drinking, in what, according to all the guidebooks, was one of the loveliest of all Cumbria's lovely campsites.

It would have worked well had the old VW not developed a mechanical problem which, to our disappointment and theirs, left it beyond immediate repair.

Tricia and I were already on the way there by the time we heard the news, so we continued, knowing that the campsite at Stonethwaite is not a place where disappointment lasts for long.

It is set in a majestic location, down a hideously bumpy track which descends into the depths of the valley, with great mountains rising steeply on either side and a river tumbling over the rocks in a succession of waterfalls, deep pools and swirling eddies. It is, quite simply, the most picturesque spot for a campsite that I have ever seen. By the time we arrived it was quite late in the day, so there was no sense in embarking on any of the long walks which are possible from the site. And anyway Tricia and I were both more than happy just to enjoy the tranquillity and splendour of the place Alison had found for us, where the silence of the mountains was broken only by the tinkling of the river and the occasional raised voice from one of the occupants of the tents which lined its nearside bank.

We did go for a walk, but only a short one, and spent most of the afternoon just sitting on a rock, gazing at the view with the river gurgling at our feet.

Only once was the serenity disturbed – when the site warden reprimanded a man for driving far too fast along the rough stone track past the children playing on the grass.

After Stonehaven it was reassuring to be back in a world of such unspoiled and "unimproved" beauty. And the fact that the approach road was too small for any over-sized motorhomes and their bolshie owners was just a bonus.

11
LANGHOLM
Scottish Borders
Friday September 12

The papers had been full of the spectacular Aurora Borealis those of us living in Scotland and Northern England would be able to enjoy. Conditions would be perfect and the display – with the "Northern Lights" flashing green, yellow and red across the sky thanks to some kind of electrical storm above the Arctic – would be visible to almost anyone who happened to be outside on the night.

I needed no more persuasion to decide my next Bongo Night would be devoted to enjoying the spectacle.

I needed somewhere dark, where the night sky would be unsullied by street lights and car headlights, and where there were plenty of places in which a man in his campervan would remain undisturbed.

A short search on Google Earth showed me that there was such a spot just a couple of miles from Langholm in the Scottish border country – on a remote hillside called Whita Hill, which faced due north and, as far as I could tell, had almost nothing between it and the North Pole.

I arrived early enough to have a look at it before it got dark, and it seemed ideal – a parking space big enough for half a dozen cars, beside a bizarre rusting iron sculpture from where energetic visitors could walk up the track to the top of the hill where an obelisk pays tribute to a distinguished local soldier and statesman called Sir John Malcolm, who died in 1833.

Sure enough, it seemed just what I was looking for . . . and the uninterrupted view northwards over the wild moorland would have made the trip worthwhile even without the prospect of the Northern Lights.

I studied the rusting sculpture (it turned out to be a memorial in the shape of an open book, dedicated to the memory of Hugh MacDiarmid, a Scottish poet and political activist who grew up in Langholm in the late 1890s), walked to the top of the hill to inspect the monument to Sir John and on my return to the car park found a small car tucked in closely beside the Bongo. The occupants – a middle aged couple with southern accents – told me they were from Essex but had spent a fortnight's holiday in the area the previous year, and had loved the place so much they had now returned to buy a house. They were spending a week house-hunting and in the meantime were camping and had come to the monument merely to exercise their dog.

I suspect they saw in me the person they would have liked to be – a man with the freedom to do as he chose, and a man who (in their imagination anyway) could jump in his campervan and travel wherever he liked in the world whenever he wanted to.

They would probably have been disappointed to learn that my next journey would be a couple of miles down the hill to the chipshop in Langholm, even though it is a charming little town and a lovely place for a gentle stroll in the parks or through the maze of back streets, all of which seem to end at the river.

Only one thing spoiled it on this night – the rain.

In my planning of this trip to see the Northern Lights I had not given much thought to the fact that it might be raining, but it was not something I could overlook now. As I sat in the Bongo, eating my chips and listening to the rain beating hard upon the roof, I realised I could not see the other side of the car park. My chances of seeing the Lights seemed remote . . .

Back on top of the hill things were even less promising. The rain had slackened off by the time I got back to my parking place, but a billowing mist had closed in, creating an impenetrable curtain between me and the Arctic Circle.

It was almost too thick to see the two women cyclists until they were almost upon me. They came up the hill from Langholm, still pedalling even though they would probably have made faster progress if they had got off and pushed. They were both, I would guess, in their 60s – one loud and brash, and so keen to invade my personal space that two or three times I had to take a step backwards to reclaim it; the other quieter and less confident, and happy to hang back and enter into the conversation only with a few nods and timid smiles.

They were, they told me, from a village near Carlisle, on the opposite side of the city from where I live, and had left their husbands at home so they could go off on a week-long cycling holiday in the Scottish Borders.

I was polite, I hope, and genuinely interested in what they were doing – and impressed that two people of that age would want to give up the comforts of home to embark of what was clearly quite a gruelling mission – but I confess it was with some relief that I watched as they eventually climbed into their saddles and pedalled off up the hill ("We'd better get going or we won't do the next ten miles before it gets dark").

The mist closed in behind them and I was fairly certain that my chances of seeing the Northern Lights had gone. Even so, I set my alarm to wake me every hour so that I could look out to see if, by some miracle, the fog had cleared and the sky was alive with flashing lights.

I woke at regular intervals until 4am, but then, seeing only grey, I accepted the inevitable, cancelled the alarm and slept soundly until I was awoken by the sound of car engines and swooshing tyres at eight.

A group of people were standing at the edge of the lay-by, most carrying the sort of small rucsacs that suggested they were planning to have a gentle ramble rather than a full-blown hike over the moors.

"Ah, good morning, are you coming to join us?" said a man in a tweed jacket.

"Er no," I replied. "Anyway, who is 'us'?"

He told me that all the people spread out before me, and a few more who hadn't arrived yet, were members of the local poetry society, who had gathered there in the lay-by for a reading of some of Hugh

McDiarmid's best poems beside his memorial since it was his birthday.

"You'd be very welcome to join us," he told me. "You like poetry, I expect."

I have no idea why he "expected" that I liked poetry, but I felt obliged to tell him that in fact I didn't, that I had never understood it (apart from the odd bit of Betjeman, which I noticed drew something of a grimace to his lips) and that my opinion of poetry echoed that expressed by a reader of the Times who, in a letter to the editor, once memorably defined poetry as "anything that's read in a funny voice".

"Oh well, maybe we could change your mind," he said. "And there'll be a wee dram at the end of it."

With this he opened his rucsac and pulled out a bottle.

"You like single malt whisky, I expect."

I told him that this time he expected right, but probably not at nine o'clock in the morning and not when I really ought to be getting home.

"Aye, maybe you're right," he said, putting the bottle back whence it had come. "It would be a bad habit to get into."

"Enjoy your poetry," I said.

"Aye, and we'll enjoy the whisky too, bad habit or no."

12
GLASSON DOCK
Lancashire
Friday September 19

My 50th season following Bristol City was turning into something of a dream. Supporting them through half a century of under achievement had not prepared me for the story now unfolding every Saturday afternoon. We were by now top of the league, still unbeaten all season and commentators (though not we fans, who after decades of having our hopes dashed, tended to be more cautious in our optimism) were talking of us as being odds on for promotion.

So the opportunity of seeing the mighty City at Fleetwood – one of the nearest League 1 clubs to my home – was obviously too good to miss.

And so was the chance of combining the match with one of my Bongo Nights.

I could, I now know, have simply driven to Fleetwood and slept in the van there, parked on the sea front, but instead I chose to break my journey at Glasson Dock, a much more attractive place than it sounds, where the ukpubstopovers.co.uk website told me the landlady of the Dalton Arms was happy to let campervans stay overnight in her car park.

I had been to Glasson Dock before and knew it to be a pretty little place, with a handful of houses, two pubs and a boatyard clustered around a small harbour guarded from the sea by a couple of huge lock gates.

I was happy to have an excuse to go there again.

I found the Dalton Arms tucked away beside the harbour, with the large car park almost hidden behind a wall, making it possible for a campervan to stay there virtually unnoticed by anyone else in the village.

I didn't like to presume that I would be welcome as an overnight guest, no matter what ukpubstopovers.co.uk had said, so I parked immediately outside the door, as if I had no such expectations.

A few people were at the bar, so it was easy enough to bring their conversation round to the Bongo – which they could see through the door – as I was ordering a pint.

"Will you be eating?" the barmaid asked.

"That depends," I told her. "It says on the internet that you let campervans park overnight here. If that's still right, then yes please. If it's not I'll just have the pint because I'd better be moving on."

The barmaid told me I would be welcome – not just welcome but "very, very welcome" in fact – to stay, though she suggested that sometime during the evening I might like to move the van to a quieter corner of the car park (which had been my intention all along).

I ordered pie and mash and peas (the menu was not extensive) and sat down at a table to read a months-out-of-date copy of Lancashire Life.

The group at the bar showed no interest in me and were busy laughing among themselves in a circle that did not invite intruders, so after finishing my pie (not the finest pub meal I've ever had, but welcome nonetheless) I followed the barmaid's advice and moved the Bongo to the far corner of the car park, taking the opportunity to make the bed while I was there, and then to have a short walk around the harbour to admire the boats.

It looked like being a long night – it was only about 7.30 and there were at least three hours yet before I could crawl into bed, so I went back into the pub determined that if the gang at the bar weren't going to talk to me I was at least going to talk to them.

Like a sheepdog picking off the lone sheep at the edge of the flock, I identified the man sitting on a high bar stool at the left hand side of the group, pushed in beside him to order another pint and turned to speak.

"Nice pub," I said.

"Tis now," he replied. "But you should have seen it a few months ago. Rubbish then. Nobody came in."

He was clearly drunk, or well on the way to being so, but at least he was someone to talk to. He told me that he was living on a canal boat in the harbour
(not an ideal location for a man who would be staggering drunkenly home at
the end of the evening, I thought), but that his real home was in a village in north Cumbria which he had no doubt I would never have heard of.

I told him that I lived in north Cumbria too, and that I knew his village well. In fact it transpired I also knew – and in one case had even once worked for – several of his friends. As I chatted with him my right ear was also tuned into the conversation of the others at the bar – a mixture of an English couple now living in Inverness, who would be returning home in the morning to vote in the Scottish independence referendum; a Scottish couple now living in Lancashire, who complained about the unfairness of not being allowed to join in the vote on their homeland's future; and a couple – both even more drunk than my new friend on the high bar stool – who had never been to Scotland and clearly never wanted to.

Having two Scottish grandchildren, a son who lives in Aberdeenshire and a daughter in Edinburgh, I felt entitled to join in their conversation and offer my thoughts on Scottish independence, though their views seemed very much influenced by the worst of the tabloid press ("I hear there's going to be a customs post at Gretna" or "They won't let me in because I haven't got a passport").

I wouldn't normally have chosen any of them as a drinking companion, but despite their initial reluctance to allow me into their circle they were friendly enough and gave me someone to talk to until closing time.

Then in turn – the couple from Inverness, then the Scots and then the drunks – they slowly took their leave and went out into the night, leaving only me and the inebriate on the bar stool. To my relief he too decided to go home, leaving just me and the barmaid. I thanked her once again, assured her that the light from the pub sign would not disturb me, and went to bed.

For the record: The next day Fleetwood Town scored first, then Bristol City scored three quick goals and were coasting to what seemed an inevitable victory until Fleetwood Town somehow managed to get two goals and were, in the end, unlucky not to win. City were still unbeaten and still top of the league.

13
TULLAGH BAY
County Donegal
Friday September 24

Tullagh Bay is a place I would never have discovered had not traumatic events once happened at home while we were away on holiday in Ireland.

We had just parked the Bongo for the night beside the sea in Connemara when we received a text from one of our friends breaking to us news of what had happened in our absence.

Memories of the incident are still too painful even today, five years after the event, for it to be discussed here, so suffice to say that the shock for Tricia and me, feeling so far away in Ireland was immense.

At a distance of 300 miles, we could not decide what to do. Should we cut our holiday short and go home to pick up the pieces there . . . or should we continue with it as best we could, knowing that whatever awaited us at home would still be there no matter when we reached it.

We slept fitfully and, in the morning, had still not decided what to do. And, to make our spirits even gloomier, the sky was black, a gale was blowing in off the Atlantic and the rain was hammering on the roof of the Bongo.

We drove on, not knowing quite where we were driving to. One minute we had decided to head straight back to the Belfast ferry, the next we were looking at the atlas to see where might offer us somewhere to park for the night.

We drove on, through the rain. We drove on for more than a hundred miles, mostly in gloomy, near-tearful silence. Then – on a dual carriageway in the (almost) very north of Ireland – I saw a sign that pointed the way to Malin Head.

"I've heard of that," I shouted. "It's on the shipping forecast. You know, Dogger, South Itsura, German Bight and all that."

I pulled the steering wheel to the left, having made the decision – based purely on those half remembered bulletins of gales and poor visibility – to give our holiday one more try.

The road took us onto the peninsula of Inishowen, a piece of the Irish Republic which, bizarrely, protrudes further north than even the most northerly point of Northern Ireland, and it opened up a part of the country still largely undiscovered by all but the people who live there. A land of spectacular beaches, wild open moorland, small mountains and lovely little villages where – as everywhere else in that glorious country – the locals really do still take time to smile at you as you drive past.

Something – I know not what, because the place was not marked on any of our maps – made me turn left off what passed as the main road, into the seaside village of Tullagh Bay and as far into the Bayside Caravan Park as the closed gate would allow us. We sat there for a while, until a small man with curly grey hair and a suntan emerged from the house beside the gate and beckoned us in.

This was Billy McVeigh.

I explained that we were just passing, apologised for what I knew must appear our rather emotional, shell-shocked appearance and said we just wanted somewhere to spend the night and collect our thoughts. I cannot describe what it was about Billy but within half an hour he was a friend, and 15 minutes after that he had heard all about what had happened at home.

He was suitably and genuinely shocked and sympathetic, but told us we had come to the right place if we needed a peaceful haven to spend the night while we decided what to do, and his unspoken understanding went a long way to calming the turmoil of our emotions.

And so did the peacefulness we found in the place: A five-minute walk took us through the sand dunes to one of the finest beaches I've ever seen – three miles of pale golden sand, along which we walked for hours, talking and wondering about the implications of what had happened.

But such was the glorious tranquillity of the place that we decided – no, that's too strong a word, we came to realise – that nothing would be gained by cutting short our holiday.

We had told Billy that we would stay for just one night, but in fact it was with heavy hearts that we left four days later. We had found a place which was so beautiful and so welcoming we did not want to leave . . . though we were certain it would not be long till we'd be back.

And so we were. My visit to Tullagh Bay for a Bongo Night in September 2014 was my fifth, though it was the first I had made without Tricia. The very act of making that journey on my own – the hundred miles from home to the ferry terminal at Cairnryan, the ship to Larne, and the lovely drive across the top of Northern Ireland to catch the smaller ferry from Magilligan to Greencastle – seemed strange, and by the time I arrived at Billy's place I was beginning to wonder whether it was really such a good idea. It wasn't being on my own that unsettled me (I'm happy enough with my own company, and anyway I had been alone for most of my best Bongo Nights), but being alone doing familiar things, in familiar places, which in the past Tricia had always been there to share with me was distinctly discomfiting.

Billy was there to welcome me. Most of his site is filled with privately owned static caravans, which people from the city of Derry use as weekend retreats or places for family holidays, so he pointed me towards the spot he had reserved for me in the area set aside for touring campervans and caravans.

The afternoon continued in the tradition set on our previous visits. I gave him, as I always did, a couple of dozen cans of Guinness bought from our local Tesco – so much cheaper, bizarrely, than those he could buy at any supermarket in Ireland – and he told me, as he always did, that he was cooking a stew which I would be welcome to share with him if I cared to call at his house a little later. I walked down to the wonderful beach (as I always did) and gulped down great lungfuls of sea air and wondered (as I always did) how it was that such a beautiful place remained so unknown by everyone apart from the handful of almost-local Irish people who looked upon it as their undiscovered secret.

Tricia and I had learned early on that very few English people ever found their way there, and it seemed the few who did were not very interested in getting to know Billy and his friends. For us, though, the people who lived there were part of Tullagh's beauty . . . and its fascination.

Billy himself is a staunch republican whose image can be seen on one of the city of Derry's famous murals – holding a brick behind his back while, as a teenager, he faced down a British Army armoured car heading towards him in the Bogside at the height of the so-called "Troubles". I know little about his past, but he has told me that he grew up with Martin McGuinness, the former IRA leader who is now deputy first minister of Northern Ireland, that he spent some time in prison in Dublin though he has never been convicted of any criminal offence, and that he abhors violence and believes that the excesses of neither the republican nor the loyalist sides can be condoned.

Alongside Billy on all our visits has been his best friend Bill McElaney, a musician who was born in the next village, but was taken by his parents to live in the USA at a very early age before returning a few years ago to buy a house just down the road from the Bay View caravan park. Bill, who started life as a special needs teacher before realising that what he really wanted to do was work as a musician, makes his living (a very good one, I suspect) playing to the huge Irish community in and around Boston, Mass, but returns whenever he can to his house in Inishowen, the place he still regards as home.

One of the highlights of our visits has always been the trip to the local pub, the marvellously named Rusty Nail, where Bill forms a scratch band – along with locals on an accordion and a tin whistle – for the sort of night of music that it seems only the Irish can produce.

On one occasion I took my banjo – on the insistence of the two Bills, despite the fact that my talent on that instrument is severely limited – and the night I spent helping to play Irish (including, let's be honest, many anti British) songs, remains one of the highlights of my life.

I would not have dared to do such a thing – to risk making a total prat of myself in front of so many people I didn't know – anywhere else but in that corner of Ireland, but there I felt among friends. The locals seemed to have taken us to their hearts as much as we had taken them to ours, and it had not been long before we had become known simply as "The English Couple", a title which somehow differentiated us from any other English couples who had come into, and gone out of, their lives, and at the Rusty Nail they welcomed me, and made allowances, and took it as a compliment that I had turned up with a banjo to join them in their feast of music.

This time, in September, I had left my banjo at home, and taken my guitar instead – on the basis that there's not much to do in a small campervan when it gets dark before six o'clock, and playing a guitar (albeit only slightly better than I play the banjo) is a good way of passing the time.

When, after demolishing his hearty and very tasty stew, Billy invited me to spend the evening with him and Bill in the "Porto" – the caravan site's Portacabin – it was inevitable that I would be asked to take my guitar.

The Porto has a few easy chairs, a television, a pool table and a fridge packed with Guinness, but, in best Irish tradition, its main purpose on such occasions is to provide a place for the playing of music.

I was glad of the invitation, because there were times during that visit to Tullagh Bay – when I had nothing in particular to do, and when Bill and Billy were busy doing other things, that I felt desperately, almost tearfully lonely.

It was a strange thing. On many of my previous Bongo Nights I had revelled in being alone, and in having glorious places entirely to myself. But here in Tullagh Bay, where I was among friends, I found it deeply troubling. The only explanation I could find was that Tullagh Bay was a place that Tricia and I had discovered together, loved together and been back to together, so it was not somewhere that I could enjoy without her.

So thank heavens for that night in the Porto. Once again the spirit of Ireland worked its magic, and I felt neither embarrassed nor self conscious singing and playing my guitar to an audience which included a man who made his living doing just that. I reckoned there was no shame in being the second best guitarist there (I knew that Billy could not play a musical instrument of any sort, and the handful of guests from the caravan site made it clear they couldn't either) and anyway I knew that the Irish way is to respect anyone just for giving it a go.

Bill and I took it in turns, both of us singing mostly Irish songs (my versions of "Nancy Spain" and "The Fields of Athenry" went down particularly well), and as the evening stretched well into the night I was not troubled by any of the loneliness which had earlier come so close to spoiling my trip.

I went to bed happy . . . and greatly looking forward to tomorrow.

14
MALIN HEAD
County Donegal
Monday September 27

Although I'd been looking forward to seeing my friends in Tullagh Bay, I suspected that my next Bongo Night would be the highlight of my trip to Ireland.

I had been to Malin Head a few times before, on our previous visits to the Inishowen peninsula, but I'd never before spent more than a couple of hours there. I knew it was a wondrously wild, atmospheric place with the sea pounding it on three sides, where the very tip of Ireland (it's ironic that the most northerly point is in fact in the Republic rather than Northern Ireland) points a defiant finger towards . . . absolutely nothing. Depending on which way you're facing – which in turn depends to a large extent on which way you've turned to escape the wind – there is nothing between you and the Arctic. Or Greenland. Or Nova Scotia. It feels like the end of the world, and indeed in many ways it is.

Which makes it no surprise that it was a place in which I had long wanted to spend the night.

As I drove the breathtakingly beautiful 20 miles north from Tullagh Bay I was excited by the idea of having such a wonderful place all to myself – an excitement troubled only by the fear that maybe I wouldn't. There might be someone else like me, who thought it a good idea to park a campervan (or, more likely, a fully fledged motorhome – some of the vans touring Ireland these days are, even on the remotest roads there, of a ridiculously extravagant size) in the very spot I had set my heart on.

I arrived to find the place bustling with day trippers. The few official parking spaces were full, every reasonably level patch of grass or rock had some sort of vehicle parked upon it, and the already narrow road was made even narrower by cars parked higgledy-piggledy along it. I drove to the top of the hill, known as Banba's Crown, where the road comes to a stop in a bell-shaped turning place next to a ruined Napoleonic fort where a mobile coffee shop and a van selling souvenirs were parked. There I managed a neat 12-point turn and tucked the Bongo into the one remaining parking space, with the nearside wheels perched precariously on a rocky shelf which – had it had been any less stable – might have crumbled and sent me tumbling sideways towards serious inconvenience and embarrassment, if not injury or death.

My plan was simple. I would lurk there for as long as it took, keeping watch over the small tarmacked area 50 yards or so back down the hill, where five cars were parked, each with its bonnet facing Newfoundland. As soon as anyone returned to any of those cars I would be ready to jump in the Bongo and make a dash down the hill to bag the space they had vacated. For two years or more I had dreamed of getting one of those spaces and I wasn't going to miss out on it through being unprepared.

In the meantime I wandered up to the top of the hill where, after ordering a hot chocolate and a slice of gooey Sicilian orange cake, I explained to the man at the coffee wagon that the only reason I kept walking away from him was to sneak a look at "my" parking place further down the road.

His name was Dominic and he and his wife Andrea ran their Caffe Banba business from the tiny village of Ballyhillion, which I had come through a few miles back on the road from Tullagh Bay. He had been working at Malin Head long enough, he said, to know that most people drove up in their cars, spent just long enough to get someone to take a photograph of them standing on a rock at the top (many of them pointing dramatically out to sea, apparently), before climbing back into their cars and driving back to wherever they had come from. Those who stayed long enough to buy a coffee were, he said, were in a disappointingly small minority, and those who opted for a walk along the magnificent clifftop path were even fewer still. His observations showed, he said, that most people chose to spend less than 15 minutes in this beautiful place.

    He was right. After ten minutes a middle-aged couple and a dog returned to a silver Skoda – which was not just one of the five cars parked down the hill, but was the one in the very spot in which I hoped to spend the night. The man opened the boot, threw in a small rucsac and followed his wife and dog into the car. By the time he started the engine I was sitting in the Bongo, and by the time his car's reversing lights came on I was slowly inching down the hill towards him. The parking space had been vacant for no more than ten seconds before I filled it. As I tugged on the handbrake and turned off the engine I was, I expect, smiling.

    My parking spot was – apart from the fact that four cars were tucked in closely beside me – all that I had imagined. The bonnet of the Bongo was indeed facing Newfoundland, with nothing between me and that faraway place except the few remaining yards of the Irish coastline and an awful lot of ocean. The sun was shining brightly, picking out the purple heather on the headland and the shining white of the breakers on the sea. The breeze, blowing warm from the west, was enough to take with it any intrusive sound of human voices from further up the hill. And, because the tide was high, the waves were crashing onto the rocks in the small bay just a short walk from where I sat.

    I accepted the invitation of the shingle path that led from the lay-by, shrugging my backpack onto my shoulders (I had already packed it with a flask of tea, a bar of fruit and nut chocolate and the slice of Sicilian orange cake) and set off towards the furthest point of the headland about a mile away to my left. Once I had descended the first sharp slope I was hidden from every other soul in the place – or, rather, they were hidden from me. I could have been the only person on the planet.

The path at Malin Head – considerably improved in the two years since I'd last been there – snakes along the north western side of the headland, taking the walker across a landscape of huge patches of heather interspersed by great peaty hags which seem to form armchairs for giants, all looking out to sea. Below, the water spewed white and bubbly over the rocks and, above, the gulls were wheeling and swooping as if in celebration of such a perfect day.

By the time I got back to the Bongo most of the other cars had gone and Dominic had wandered away from his coffee wagon and found himself a better view of the sea. He grinned at me as I approached.

"Happy now?" he asked. "I told you you'd eventually have it to yourself and sure enough you will."

I now recognised him as the same man who had served Tricia and me coffee on our visit two years before, and he said he remembered me too (though I think he must have only been being friendly). He told me he had had a good summer there, making a decent enough living serving hot drinks and cake to the steady stream of trippers who came, took their photographs . . . but seldom stayed.

He had already spotted where I had parked.

"You will be all right down there," he said. "You won't be disturbed."

He told me that earlier in the year I might have had two or three other campervans keeping me company, but (he didn't put it in quite these words) in the middle of September nobody else would be daft enough to want to spend a night in as bleak a place as Malin Head.

This reassured me for two reasons: It was obviously acceptable for campervans to park up overnight there and nobody who had parked there in the past had been disturbed by the locals – if there were any – so nobody would come banging on my door in the middle of the night to tell me I had no right to be there.

I sat on a rock on the top of the hill, watching contentedly as one by one the last of the trippers decided they had seen enough, climbed back into their cars and drove back to somewhere more civilised.

At six o'clock Dominic packed up his coffee wagon for the day and drove off, giving me a cheery wave as he went. That left just two vehicles – the Bongo and a dark blue BMW which had arrived a few minutes before and, despite there being numerous other spaces to choose from that late in the afternoon, had tucked itself closely in beside it. A family – mum, dad and three excited children – piled out, looked at the view, probably not realising they were looking towards Nova Scotia, and chased each other to the old fort at the top. There they had another look at the view, before chasing each other down again, jumping breathless into their car . . . and driving off. They had been at Malin Head for approximately seven and a half minutes.

And then I was alone. I had that spectacularly beautiful place to myself, and it was just as magical as I had dreamed it would be. I sat on a rock beside the Bongo, looking out at nothing – or, maybe looking out at everything – and I confess I had tears in my eyes.

As the sun fell down over the sea – it just had to be a beautiful sunset – I went for another walk, back to the top of the hill and then down another well-made path for a second circuit of the headland as the sea and the sky both turned a fiery red.

I returned in the near-dark to find that a couple – German, by their accents – had parked beside the Bongo. They gave me a friendly greeting but soon, without ever walking more than five yards from their car, drove off.

As the tail lights of their car disappeared into the distance I pulled open a can of Guinness, then in less than five minutes rustled up a quick and surprisingly tasty supper of noodles in sweet and sour sauce. I was inside the van, tucking into the feast, when I heard voices.

Six people, only two of them with torches, emerged out of the gloom, up the path from the headland. The one in front, a woman of about 30, "ooohed" in surprise when she spotted the Bongo. She shone her torch at it, sweeping the whole van in one movement from bonnet to tail – and therefore picking me out as I downed the last forkful of noodles – before returning the beam swiftly for a closer inspection of the lilac dragonfly stickers that decorate most of the front.

"Ooooh," she said again. "That's really cool. What a cool van! I want one!"

I'm always happy to talk to anyone who likes my Bongo, so I climbed out, thanking her for her kind comments, telling her that it was indeed a cool van and commiserating with her that she didn't have one like it. Her five friends were polite, but it was plain that they did not quite share her enthusiasm for the Bongo – not at that time of night, when it was dark and they clearly still had some way to walk, anyway – but she refused to leave until I had given her a tour of the inside of the van.

"Cool," she said. "Really cool."

And as they left, continuing on their way, to (I imagined) the nearest village, which was still at least another three miles away, I heard her voice fading into the night. "Cool. Really cool. Want one. Cool. Lucky."

It was eight o'clock, dark apart from the stars and I was alone in paradise again.

I fetched my guitar from the Bongo and sat on a rock overlooking the sea. I sang 'One Small Star', a song Eric Bogle wrote after the massacre of 16 children and a teacher at Dunblane Primary School in Scotland in 1996. 'When I need to feel you near me/I come to this quiet place/With the silver light of countless stars/Falling on my face.' Somehow it felt appropriate. And so did the tears in my eyes.

There had not seemed much point putting the blinds down when I went to bed so I was woken by the rising sun shining onto my pillow. For a moment, sleepily, I wondered where I was. But then I heard the waves crashing onto the rocks below . . . and I remembered. I got up quickly, partly because I wanted to make the most of having the place to myself and partly because I knew that sooner or later I would need – if not a lavatory with flushing toilet, wash-hand basin and a six-month-old copy of Readers Digest – a hole in the ground in some spot discreetly away from the first arriving tourists. It was almost 50 years since I'd last crapped in the open air (that was when I was celebrating the end of my A-levels with a trek across Dartmoor) but I had at least come prepared – Go Outdoors do a very good fold-up spade for less than a tenner.

So my third walk along that magnificent coastline was in search of a suitable piece of peatbog (easy both to dig a hole in and to squat on, I thought) out of sight of any watching trippers. It was only after the mission had been accomplished that I realised how needless my walk had been. Who was around to watch me? Nobody for about five miles. It was the most beautiful walk to a toilet I've ever had!

It was almost another three hours, long after ten o'clock, before I saw my first human that day. By that time I'd had Malin Head – glorious, beautiful, wild, magical, spiritual Malin Head – to myself for nearly 14 hours. It was everything I'd hoped for, and much much more than I'd had any right to expect.

The first person I saw was a man who arrived in a battered old car with his two dogs, which he took for a run around the Napoleonic fort. Then a couple of very fit young men on bicycles, who cycled up the hill, ate a quick high-energy biscuit and cycled down again. Then another man with a dog and – the first of the day trippers – a couple with a baby who smiled at me as they passed. And then a procession of other cars, most of whose occupants, true to form, spent no more than ten minutes there.

I admit I felt aggrieved that these people had seen fit to invade the place I'd come to feel was mine, but equally I realised that I'd had more than my share of it. These people might see it in the middle of the morning, take their photographs on top of the hill and even for a moment appreciate the true majesty of the place . . . but they'd not seen it at sunset, they'd not known it in the dark, they'd not witnessed the sunrise, they'd not had it all to themselves and they'd not sat on a rock and sung songs to the stars.

When Dominic brought his coffee wagon back at noon I was languishing in that unsettling feeling of anticlimax that comes when something truly special comes to an end. It was Sunday morning – and, by now, a wet Sunday morning, at that – and I wasn't booked on the ferry to go home until Wednesday. What was I going to do till then, other than continue my feeling of disappointment?

I walked to the top of the hill for a coffee (I hadn't bothered to make one in the Bongo for breakfast, knowing that I'd soon be able to have one made for me) and joined the queue – yes, a queue! – at Dominic's van, whose sign proclaims that it's "Ireland's most northerly coffee shop". Ahead of me was a jolly lady, about the same age as me, who I took to be American.

"No, Canadian," she told me. She was on a tour of Ireland with a group of friends, had seen Dublin, Belfast, the Antrim Glens and the Giant's Causeway, but still had the whole of the west coast to do, including such favourite places as Galway, Killarney and the Ring of Kerry. But now she just wanted to go home.

I discovered that there in that wild place, in a queue for a coffee in one of the world's most unlikely coffee shops, I had found, in Sheila, the lady from New Brunswick, a kindred spirit. We talked for a long time, and to hell with the rain that by now was beginning to run down our necks.

We spoke of the magic of Malin, the spirituality we had found in its majestic scenery, the special feeling we got when we looked out knowing there was nothing in front of us but 3,000 miles of ocean, and we registered astonishment at the soul-less people who stay there for no longer than the time it takes to park a car and take a photograph.

"I've been to some wonderful places in Ireland," she told me. "But there's been nothing as good as this."

She had, quite simply, fallen in love with Malin Head, just as I had. And now she had been there and savoured it and loved it, she just wanted to go home.

"Nothing is going to compare with this," she said. "Nothing's even going to come close. So I want to go home right now, this minute."

I smiled at her. "Thank you," I said. "That's exactly how I feel but I hadn't realised it. Yes, I want to go home now too."

I paused to buy some cheap souvenirs from the mobile gift shop – some seaweed bath salts and a candle for Tricia, and an "I've been to Malin Head" magnet for the Bongo – then walked down the hill, found my mobile phone and sent a text message to Tricia.

"Just tearing myself from Malin Head in the rain," I said. "Absolutely nothing will beat that – apart from coming home of course – so I'm coming home. Should see you tomorrow if I can get a ferry."

15
ORTON SCAR
Cumbria
Tuesday October 7

I can never go to Orton, a village a few miles south of Penrith in Cumbria, without thinking of Prince Charles.

I think it was because he had some very kind things to say about the farmers' market there when he visited it many years ago – soon after I had moved to Cumbria from the East Midlands and back in the days when farmers' markets were so new that I hardly knew what they were.

These days I know it as a pretty little village on the fringes of the Pennines, a village Tricia and I walked through on the Coast to Coast Walk more than 20 years ago, which is just a couple of miles from some dramatic limestone outcrops whose wildflowers make them quite wonderful to walk through on a sunny summer's day.

There was no hint of summer – nor of Prince Charles either – when I passed through it on the way to my 15th Bongo Night.

The drizzle which had started almost as soon as I'd left home was still falling gently as I drove out of Orton and up the hill towards the area known as Orton Scar. There were a couple of potential wildcamping sites there, and my plan was to get parked in one of them early enough for me to go for a walk before it got dark, and I confess I had expected to be able to do that in bright sunshine (I am always optimistic when I set off on a Bongo Night, no matter how grisly the forecast might be).

I found a lay-by at the top of the hill – the sort of place middle-aged ladies go to walk their dogs, or travelling animal feed salesmen stop for a flask of tea on their way to their next stop at some local farm. But there was no sign of any bright sunshine.

I pulled in and parked beside a couple of empty cars and was immediately joined by another, driven by a rotund young woman who carefully opened a neat white box on the seat beside her and enthusiastically demolished four cream cakes before starting her engine again and driving off. She had not got out of her car, nor, as far as I could tell, interrupted her feast to look at the view.

I was determined to make rather more of my surroundings, so went for a walk despite the rain. A track – rocky and uneven, but good enough for a vehicle – led from the lay-by, further onto the fell and deeper into the limestone pavement. After a quarter of a mile or so it widened out into what would have been an excellent overnight parking spot for a wildcamping campervan.

I was tempted. The lay-by down by the road was good enough . . . but this one, out of sight of the road and indeed of every other sign of human habitation, was undoubtedly better.

For a moment I wanted to walk back to fetch the Bongo, to bring it up to this most magical of wild places, but as I made my way back down the track I realised that, while it would have been a truly wonderful place to spend the night, it was just a bit too wild, a bit too isolated and a bit too out of sight. My primary criterion for safe camping, I reminded myself, was always to leave myself an escape route. Apart from the dogging lay-by on the way to Sheffield (which did not count because I had felt obliged to leave there more out of embarrassment than fear) I had never yet had cause to make a quick exit from any Bongo spot, but there was always the chance, however remote, that some ne'er-do-well – some passing drunk, thief or thug – might think it a good idea to target a small campervan parked in a remote spot, so I never liked to stop in a place from which I could not get out fast in an emergency. And that spot, beautiful though it was, on top of the limestone pavement on Orton Scar, could be reached only along the stone track, and if that was blocked I would be trapped.

I decided, with a heavy heart, to leave the Bongo where it was. It was perfectly good enough. And it would be safe.

The rain played me a gentle lullaby as it drummed on the Bongo roof and I slept like a log until people began to arrive in their cars to give their dogs their early morning exercise. I like to think they looked at me with envy as they were welcomed by the faint smell of cooking bacon wafting over the countryside.

16
MARTINDALE
Cumbria
Tuesday October 14

My younger son Will often recounts his adventures as a deckhand on the Ullswater steamers in the Lake District – tourists not knowing which side of the boat to get off ("We normally recommend the side nearest the jetty, madam"); tourists asking how, if the compass points north, the captain knows where south is; tourists asking if the islands have to be weighted down "to stop them floating away".

But on this occasion he was telling me that his boat had narrowly missed a red deer stag as it swam across the bay near the landing stage at Howtown, on the eastern shore of the lake.

"Good grief, I'd forgotten!" I said. "It's the rutting season."

If you're not familiar with these parts you probably don't know that the rutting season – the time of year when great herds of red deer meet on the fells, with the stags roaring spectacularly as they go in search of a mate – has become something of an attraction. Visitors troop in their hundreds to some of the valleys where this great spectacle occurs.

One of the best places to witness it is Martindale, a remote valley hidden away down a three-mile long cul-de-sac on the eastern side of

Ullswater.

It was obviously to Martindale that Will's stag was heading as it dragged itself dripping out of the water at Howtown. And, with my memory suitably jogged, it was to Martindale that I headed for my sixteenth Bongo Night.

The road alongside that side of the lake – past a couple of campsites in which there's scarcely space to swing a tent peg in high summer, past the opulent Sharrow Bay Hotel where Paul McCartney conducted his ill-fated wooing of Heather Mills, and past the bay where Will saw the still-dripping stag – is a fine spot for wildcamping. As the road rises in a steep Z-bend, up the flanks of Harter Fell, there are several places where a small campervan can safely pull in for the night. But the best one comes a little further on, just as the road begins its descent to the little village of Sandwich.

Here, on the right, just opposite the tiny new church of Martindale (the old one is a little further down into the valley) is a rough lay-by – big enough for half a dozen cars. It's a perfect spot for a campervan – beautiful views in all directions, sheltered from any wind that might come roaring up the valley and on the sort of road that's unlikely to see any traffic once it gets dark. And, to my surprise, it's also in range of both mobile phone and digital radio (though another few yards further on will plunge you out of range of both).

It was a perfect, peaceful spot . . . and the only noise to break the silence was the distant roar of a single stag somewhere up on the fells at three o'clock in the morning.

I was awoken by a flashing orange light and the sound of heavy diesel engines. It was just after 6am and I had been joined by a Cumbria County Council highways department lorry, a mechanical shovel and three men who, with their Thermos flasks and Tupperware boxes, appeared to be having a picnic in the middle of the road. It was a relief to find that they paid not the slightest bit of attention to either me or the Bongo.

Once the picnic was done, they climbed aboard their vehicles and headed down the hill, further towards the valley where, I was certain, at that very moment the stags (apart from the one which had been bellowing most of the night) would be rising from their slumbers to greet me.

I arrived at the furthest end of the road leading into the valley after breakfast, just as the Highways Men were turning their vehicles round after filling a single pothole with steaming black tar.

I dived for the verge (partly to get out of their way and partly because that's where I had intended to park anyway) and wound down my window.

"Will I be in your way if I park here?" I asked as the lorry pulled alongside.

"Nah, you're all right," the driver called back.

"And will I get trapped up here if you're working on the road further back down the valley later on?"

"Nah, you're still all right. We're finished for the day."

I put on my walking clothes, packed my rucsac with a bottle of drink and a banana, and headed for the track leading up the valley, wondering what sort of job it was that started at six o'clock in the morning and was finished by eight.

I now had the valley to myself and, as if to prove the point, as I pushed open the gate that led onto the open moorland the stags on the fells ahead of me began roaring a welcome. At first the noise – surely one of the most evocative sounds in all of nature – came from the hill in front of me, and I could just about make out the stags there, all wide shoulders and huge antlers, but soon, as I made my way up the valley, they were joined by others on the hills closer to me, so that by the time I had been walking for about 20 minutes the roaring came from three sides, and after I'd walked a little further it closed in behind me too, so that I was surrounded by it.

This extraordinary quadraphonic sound continued as I made my way to the stony outcrop where I planned to spend my morning, and it continued almost unabated for the almost two hours that I sat on a rock marvelling at it.

Being alone in such a place, in such circumstances, can make a man selfish and proprietorial and so it was with me. This beautiful valley, with its wonderful sights and incredible sounds, was for a couple of hours mine. So when, in the distance, I saw the first other humans coming up the track, I knew my time was up. I had no appetite for sharing my valley with anyone else.

So I picked up my rucsac and started back for the Bongo.

I was friendly enough when I met the walkers – a middle aged couple and their daughter who, they told me, had just been taken on as an apprentice with the Cumbria Wildlife Trust – but I couldn't help making the point that until then I had had the valley
to myself (and, by inference, that I was not best pleased to have my aloneness disturbed by anyone else).

"Was it wonderful?"
the father asked. "I bet it was. I'd hoped we were early enough to be the
first people here so I
admit I was a bit disappointed when I saw your van already parked."

I left them without telling them that the stags were now making much less
noise than they had been two hours before,
and the last I saw of them they were spreading a blanket on the rock I had only just vacated, with their binoculars trained on a handful of deer on a far hill on which not long before there had been dozens.

Further down the valley I was happy to see further evidence that it had been a wise decision to leave when I had.

I knew a group from the Wednesday Walkers club from Brampton – the small market town a couple of miles from where I live – would be arriving sometime during the day, because my friend Betty, who is a member and the most enthusiastic fellwalker I know, had told me so. So when I saw a party of more than a dozen heading towards me I guessed that this was them.

Betty was about fourth in the line, and the others looked vaguely surprised when I grasped her in my arms and gave her a big hug. She told me that they would be walking up over The Knott and Raven Cragg (no sitting on a rock for them!).

Now, I have a love-hate relationship with walking groups like theirs. I have many friends – heavens, I'm even married to one – who relish sharing their love of the fells with other like-minded folk, so good luck to them and I sincerely hope they enjoy it. But for me, walking is something best done alone. How can you be alone with your thoughts, how can you get lost in the majesty of your surroundings, how can you enjoy every last sound and smell, when you have to walk at someone else's pace, and engage them in a conversation you don't want just so they don't realise what a miserable old git you are?

I told Betty and any of her walking friends who wanted to listen that they should have been there at eight o'clock because that was when the stags had been at their most impressive.

I counted eighteen walkers, straggled out along the path with their walking poles and rucsacs and garishly coloured cagoules.

"Thank God, I'm not with them," I thought.

Seeing them confirmed all I'd ever thought about walking in a group – it is to be avoided at all costs.

17
WALLTOWN CRAGS
Northumberland
Friday October 31

It was the wettest, windiest night of the winter so far and I was, to be frank, not in the mood for a night's Bongoing. There seemed a very good argument in favour of staying at home by the fire, sipping a favourite malt whisky and going to bed with Tricia under a warm and soft duvet. But duty called.

There were several reasons why I settled on Walltown Crags on Hadrian's Wall. It was one of my favourite places, for a start; I knew there was a good place where I could park the Bongo overnight without fear of disturbance; I would have an awe-inspiring walk in the morning (if it ever stopped raining); and – best of all – it was only about 15 miles from home, so I could leave the comforts of home quite late at night, with the Bongo bed made and (and this was a first) with me already in my pyjamas.

I could, I'm sure, have parked in the official Hadrian's Wall car park without transgressing too many jobsworth regulations, but instead I chose a wild road nearby, that ran parallel to the wall and about 100 metres from it. It felt remote, but wasn't, and it seemed extraordinary that I could be so close to – and yet isolated from – a busy world that I knew so well. As I sat in the van before going to bed I was able to watch the lights of the traffic on the A69 Carlisle to Newcastle road, coming down the hill to Greenhead less than a mile away, on a journey that I had done literally hundreds of times myself.

Although I was probably close enough to be kept awake by the noise of the traffic, that sound was wiped out by the weather and instead I was lulled to sleep by the gentle rhythm of the rain beating on the roof.

I awoke to find the bad weather had passed and the Bongo was already being picked out by a shaft of early morning sun.

After breakfast I walked over the open moorland, climbed the hill up to the wall and marvelled at the views. To the north, mile upon mile of wilderness, stretching all the way to – and well beyond – the Scottish border; to the east, the magnificent view of Hadrian's Wall snaking across the escarpment towards Newcastle; to the west, the rolling countryside towards Carlisle and the Solway plain; and to the south the dramatic outline of the Pennines.

How glad I was that I had dragged myself away from home the previous night. Early morning in such a place – standing on top of a hill in the sunshine almost before the rest of the world was stirring – was a treasure well worth sacrificing the comforts of a night at home for.

18
LATRIGG
Cumbria
Wednesday November 5

My Bongo Nights were becoming a stiffer challenge now that we had hit winter. There is, after all, not a lot to do in a small campervan once it gets dark, even in these days of digital radio to listen to, LED lights to read by and laptop computers to play DVDs on until the battery gives out.

So on Bonfire Night it made sense to spend my Bongo Night in some place where I could pass some time watching someone else's fireworks display.

The obvious place was Latrigg, a lovely wild fell which overlooks the Lake District town of Keswick, with views better than might be expected from a hill which, in truth, isn't much of a hill at all. It's the sort of hill where families go to give their small children their first taste of fell-walking – a huge green mound of a place, with a gravel path leading about half a mile to a viewpoint which provides fine views over Keswick to Derwentwater and the fells behind.

I reckoned that if anywhere was going to provide me with an evening's entertainment it would be Latrigg.

In fact November 5 was one of the most spectacularly beautiful of all Cumbria's beautiful days of the early winter – so beautiful that I left home early, in time to enjoy some of the Lake District sunshine along the way.

Although I had been to Latrigg before, I could not remember much about the car park – especially whether much of it was level enough to afford me a comfortable night's sleep – so I wanted to take a good look at it before it got dark, so I knew where to aim for later on.

I timed my journey so that I arrived on Latrigg in the middle of the afternoon, and was surprised to find the car park full. I managed to pull the Bongo onto the verge further down the road, but walked back to check the ground for a level overnight parking space in the hope that all the cars would be gone by the time I needed it. From there I continued walking through the gate on the path that led onto the open fell, and wound round in a direction I reckoned to be leading me to the place from which I would be able to look down over Keswick.

I had forgotten what a fine viewpoint it was, looking over not just the town of Keswick, but the whole length of Derwentwater and to the fells of Catbells and the Newlands Round beyond.

I sat on a bench there, just enjoying the peace, and had it to myself until a wild-looking man appeared from along a small path I had not even noticed. Alongside him, with his bushy hair and straggly beard, I felt almost trim and well turned-out.

He told me he lived in Keswick, and made the 90-minute walk up the hill and back almost every day, whatever the weather.

"You don't get many days as good as this, mind," he said. "It might not look like it but it can get quite rough sometimes, even here."

We both stayed to watch the sunset, then left in opposite directions – he back to his cosy house in the town, and I back to the car park, where I was happy to see that most of the cars had gone, leaving only a couple of stragglers and a campervan which was parked neatly in the corner by the wall.

I spent the early evening in Keswick, in the Alhambra cinema – a delightfully old fashioned place, which reminded me of the cinemas of my childhood. By the time the film finished I reckoned it was time to buy myself some fish and chips and head back to Latrigg to watch the fireworks. When I got there I discovered I had the car park to myself . . . apart from the small campervan parked in the corner. I parked well away from it and got out to walk to the viewpoint, taking a torch although it was unnecessary because of the splendid full moon that bathed the hill in a silver-blue glow.

I was just a few minutes too late. I reached the bench in time to see one rocket sending its cascade of red and blue sparks over the Keswick skyline . . . and then nothing. People there obviously held their firework parties earlier than I thought.

Even so, the twinkling lights of the town made an incredibly atmospheric scene, with the great dark bulk of the high fells behind, and as I slowly made my way back to the Bongo I was only mildly disappointed that I had seen so few fireworks. As I did so I saw the shapes of two people, one crouching and the other jumping up and down, as if to keep warm.

I discovered they were a young couple, he from one nearby village and she from another, just coming to the end of their own private firework display on the side of Latrigg. They asked me if I'd like some sparklers (the only fireworks they had left), and we spent a happy few minutes drawing crazy patterns with them in the night sky.

I returned to the Bongo, happy that Bonfire Night had not quite passed me by after all.

19
CALDBECK
Cumbria
Friday November 14

Caldbeck is a charming village on the northern edge of the Lake District, famous most of all for being the birthplace of John Peel (the huntsman who inspired the song, not the radio disc jockey), and the starting point of a couple of not-too-strenuous walks.

More important as far as my Bongo Nights are concerned, is that it boasts a decent pub and, just a couple of miles away, a host of fine overnight parking places on the common land where local farmers keep their sheep. I had always had it in mind as somewhere to wildcamp sometime, and it shot to the top of my list when I received an email from Pat and Eddie, old friends who I hadn't seen for several years.

Eddie is an expert glider pilot, and he was one of the many instructors who had tried – and eventually, after five years, succeeded – to teach me to fly (thanks to their combined efforts I had one memorable solo flight before deciding I no longer had the time, the money or the motivation to carry on with what in other circumstances could easily have become an obsessive hobby).

Their children happened to have been at the same school as ours, but we did not meet them till afterwards, when Pat in particular became a big supporter of my son Will as he started making a small name for himself in the local music world.

It was Pat who got in touch after reading about my Bongo adventures on Facebook, reminding me that she and Eddie had a campervan – a VW Celeste – which they had bought in Cornwall and suggesting that we should meet and compare notes.

Knowing that they lived just a few miles from Caldbeck, I suggested a meeting in that village's pub, the Oddfellows Arms, from which, I said, I would head off for a night on the Common.

It's always good meeting old friends and finding that, despite the years, you still get on just as well as you ever did.

And so it was with Pat and Eddie.

We found we had much more in common than we thought – not just school, gliding and campervanning, but mutual experiences and friends, one of whom, John, had worked as a blacksmith in Caldbeck until he and his new wife moved to one of the most remote communities on the western coast of Scotland.

It turned out that Eddie had known John for far longer than I had, not least because they had had a mutual love of vintage motorbikes and had been on several rallies together, each riding his ancient bike across the wild roads of their part of northern England. Eddie had lost touch with John at about the same time as we had found him, so was fascinated to hear how we had come to know him after he moved in with our friend Judy, whose own marriage had ended some time before.

John and Judy, having nowhere else to live, set up home in a barn – not a barn conversion, but a proper barn, with straw bales, cobwebs and chickens running around the floor – and used to come to our house once a week for a bath (we left a bottle of wine and two glasses in the bathroom for them), a meal and a good laugh. This continued for several months until John and Judy moved to a smallholding on Morvern, a peninsula north of Oban in Argyll, which lies down a 40-mile cul-de-sac, which itself is reached by a small ferry.

We helped them move, and I remember on that day standing in their new kitchen and being seized by a panic attack as I looked out of the window and realised just how far away I was from anywhere that mattered. I had always thought I would enjoy living in some remote place, with no neighbours for miles and nothing but wonderful views all around, but when I found it (or, rather, when John and Judy did) I discovered that it scared me to death.

We had visited John and Judy several times in the years since – once when we had slept in the Bongo in their farmyard – but Pat and Eddie told me they had tried to do so only once, and they had come away unable to find them because they had only a rough idea of where they lived.

Over our pints in the Oddfellows Arms we all agreed that we would in future make more effort to see our old friends at their Scottish hideaway.

But for now it was Caldbeck Common that called.

I followed Pat and Eddie to the parking spot they reckoned to be the best – a level area big enough for a dozen cars, well off the road and with, on a clear day, stupendous views over to the higher Lake District fells.

It seemed an ideal place to spend the night . . . I slept for a good hour, but was woken after a while by distant shouting, and the twin sounds of a revving engine and fiercely spinning tyres. I looked out and saw dancing lights on the horizon and it seemed that someone was trying to drive across the Common. At midnight. On ground that was sodden and slippery after days of rain! I went back to sleep, knowing there was nothing I could do to help even if I wanted to.

An hour later I was awake again, this time after three cars arrived and lined up side by side on the far side of my parking spot. They made very little noise, it's true – in fact they almost tiptoed in over the gravel – but their very presence was a little disturbing, as any such thing is disturbing at dead of night when you're wild camping. However there was no surreptitious opening and closing of car doors, and no flashing of headlights as there had been in the dogging lay-by above Holmfirth, and anyway after so many Bongo Nights I was getting used to all this. At the start, back in June, I would have been wide awake, ears keened for any sound, ready to react to any hint of danger or unwelcome intrusion, but now, after more experience of the things people get up to in the middle of the night, I was more relaxed about it all, and more prepared to let them get on with whatever they liked as long as it did not directly involve me.

After 15 minutes or so the three engines started up again, and my visitors crept away as quietly as they had come. What they had been doing I had no idea. And frankly I didn't much care.

In the sunshine of the morning I had the place to myself, so I went for my customary post-breakfast walk, heading determinedly – or, rather, nosily – in the direction of the midnight revving engine. Sure enough, I found deep tyre marks in the mud, surrounded by a multitude of footprints. They were on what might once have been a track, it's true, but it was a track that did not seem to be going anywhere, and which had clearly not been used for many years. Again, what they had been doing I could not guess, and again I didn't much care.

I continued my walk over the common, picking my way through the grown-over scars of some ancient quarries, and completed a circle before arriving back at the Bongo to find a car being parked rather closer to it than was strictly necessary.

The driver gave me the look of someone who was not used to having to share the place with anyone else.

I smiled and wished him good morning. He ignored me.

20
LEOMINSTER
Herefordshire
Friday November 21

Call me an old romantic, but when I was taking the Bongo on a trip to see my mother in Somerset, there was only one place to spend the night on the way – Leominster, the Herefordshire market town where Tricia and I were married in 1973.

There are many reasons for people to visit Leominster – its magnificent Priory Church (complete with historic ducking stool) where Tricia's father was vicar, and where he married us all those years ago, its quaint lanes and black and white timbered buildings, its antique shops . . . but the thing that most attracted me to it on this occasion (apart from nostalgia and the fact that it's a handy stop-off place on the way to Weston-super-Mare) was its car park.

The Leominster town car park has the distinction of being one of the very few that I've found in England that actually seems to welcome campervans. It is set on an old cattle market, in the shadow of the priory, and every evening fills up with dozens of lorries as an overnight truck stop. And there is no suggestion that campervans can't join them. The public toilets – never sparkling clean, but always acceptable, in my experience – are even left open all night.

I arrived there quite late at night, with the car park turned orange by the street lights that glistened in the puddles, and, just for old time's sake, chose a place in the far corner, as close as I could get to the church.

There was no sign of life among the wagons sharing the car park with me – in fact, there was no sign of life anywhere at all – but this was Leominster, Tricia's old home town, in which I had many happy memories, so I went for a walk. It was drizzling, the pavements were wet and the only other people about were a few
drunks stumbling home from the pubs. A police car crept past, its two occupants viewing me with suspicion, a couple of kids were snogging enthusiastically on the corner by the newsagents' shop where Tricia used to work and a woman in a very short skirt
was throwing up on the cobbles.

Back in the Bongo, tucked up beneath a thick warm duvet, I thought how good it was to be back in the town which had played such a big part in my life.

It was, though, not the most sensible of places in which to expect a good night's sleep in a campervan. In a brightly lit car park? Next to a fleet of lorries which roared into life for an early start in the small hours? Beneath a church whose clock chimed loudly every 15 minutes – and which rang out a hymn tune every hour?

I didn't sleep very well in Leominster.

21
THE STRETTON HILLS
Shropshire
Tuesday November 25

While it is perfectly possible to drive home from Weston-super-Mare in not much more than five hours, it's an unpleasant 296-mile journey up the motorway, so when I get the opportunity I like to take a scenic route and stop off on the way, particularly if I'm in the Bongo.

On a previous trip to Somerset, years before, I had found a superb wildcamping spot on the Stretton Hills above Church Stretton in Shropshire. It was a perfectly flat, tarmacked area, big enough for three or four cars, with spectacular views over the hills and towards the escarpment from where members of the Long Mynd gliding club enjoy some of the finest non-powered flying in Britain. No wonder I was so keen to use it again on the way back from the West Country this time.

It was, though, a filthy night and my "scenic" route back up the A49 through Hereford and Leominster turned into a nightmare of teeming rain, patches of fog . . . and a diversion of many miles to avoid an overturned lorry.

The village of Church Stretton was cloaked in mist, but that was nothing compared with the blanket of fog that descended as I gained a little height and climbed towards my Bongo spot in the hills. I could barely pick out the road ahead of me and nearly overshot the parking space, even though it was marked out by a couple of white posts.

   Conditions became even worse overnight, with rain pounding on the roof and the Bongo swaying in the wind, and in the morning when I pulled back the curtain to admire the view I could see . . . nothing. The lovely view over the hills was obliterated by a dirty beige fog. I could hardly see the edge of the parking place let alone the hills half a dozen miles away.

   I sat there having breakfast, hoping that by some miracle the fog would clear, even though the weather forecast on the radio had warned me that such a thing was unlikely. The whole of the West Midlands was immersed in it, and it seemed I was, quite literally, in the thick of it.

   I started the engine, reversed out and slowly picked my way back down the bendy hill to Church Stretton.

   It should have taken me about four hours to get home from there. But it took me six.

22
DRIMNIN
Scotland
Friday November 28

After my evening in the pub at Caldbeck with Pat and Eddie we all had plans that one day we would go up to visit our friends John and Judy at their remote home on the West Coast of Scotland. Sadly we never got the chance.

With a hideous irony, within a fortnight of discovering that John was a mutual friend, we heard that he was desperately ill in hospital in Inverness. Two days later we learned that his life support machine had been turned off and that he had died.

In normal circumstances Tricia and I would have stayed at his house, as we had before, but that was clearly not an option for his funeral because it would be full of his family and other friends, so Judy suggested we could park the Bongo there instead.

John's funeral – a humanist ceremony in the village hall – was followed by a burial in the local cemetery on top of the hill. We walked there behind his coffin, up a bumpy track and over a grassy field and he was laid to rest in what must be one of the loveliest cemeteries in the world – a beautiful place on top of the hill, with views over the Sound of Mull towards the village of Tobermory on the island of Mull.

That night we parked the Bongo on the track leading to John and Judy's house, so woke up to almost the same view.

I cooked breakfast in the van, and carried it in to the house, where various friends and members of John's family devoured it in the kitchen.

"Will you be counting this as one of your Bongo Nights?" Judy's daughter asked.

"I hadn't thought of it, but no," I told her. "I don't think that would be right. Bad taste almost."

"But you must!" she said. "He'd want you to. He'd want to be part of it, it's just his sort of thing."

Judy nodded.

"He'd love it," she said.

And so it is: Bongo Night No 22 was the night we spent looking out towards Tobermory after our friend John's funeral.

23
LOCH LOMOND
Scotland
Monday December 1

The idea for the next Bongo Night came the moment our neighbour Mel told me she had to fly out for a two-day business conference in Dublin. She would be flying from Glasgow airport on one day and coming back to it late on the next, which would be no problem except that her eyesight problems make it unpleasant for her to drive home in the dark.

To a man always on the look-out for interesting places to take his Bongo, the answer seemed obvious – I would drive Mel to the airport, spend the next 36 hours in or around Glasgow and come home after picking her up again.

A study of the wildcamping.co.uk website told me that, while overnight spots in the city of Glasgow itself were few and far between, there were plenty just beyond. And the one that appealed to me most was near Loch Lomond, on the road that leads through Glen Douglas and on to Loch Fyne.

That suited me very well: It was only about 30 miles from Glasgow airport, and in a part of the country I knew, but not so well that I was bored with it. To get to it I had to pass through Dumbarton, a town that boasted a small museum which I had long intended to visit. And best of all it left me a full day before returning to the airport, which I could spend catching up with an old friend whom I had not seen since we worked together in Nottingham nearly 30 years before.

The Dumbarton museum is one of two sites of the Scottish Maritime Museum. Set in buildings at the old Denny Brothers shipyard (they built the Cutty Sark among other fine vessels) it was a place I had meant to visit for years, but this was the first time I'd had an easy opportunity to do so. Its main claim to fame is the "Denny Tank" – a tank the length of a football pitch in which model ships were sailed to test the effectiveness of various hull designs – but another almost equally extraordinary one could be said to be its café, where I got a splendid meal of macaroni cheese, salad, garlic bread, apple crumble, custard and a pot of tea, all for less than a fiver.

I spent much longer in the museum than I expected, and returned to the Bongo in pouring rain, only to find that the vital key from the battery isolator had fallen out of my pocket. I had fitted the isolator as an anti theft device, having learned my lesson from the fate of my first Bongo a couple of years before, and the key – a big red plastic thing – was what was needed to complete the electrical circuit so power could reach the starter from the battery.

Without one the Bongo would simply not go.

I searched the car park, I searched the path to the museum and – with the help of several of the staff there – I searched the museum itself, all to no avail.

The museum staff were very sympathetic when I explained the problem, and a good deal more anxious than I was.

"It's just as well I've got a spare," I told them.

And so I had. Knowing that sooner or later I would lose the key, I had taken the precaution of hiding another one in a place where, I reckoned, not even the most determined car thief would find it, so much to the relief of my new friends in the museum I was able to continue my journey without too much trouble. Just as long as I didn't lose the "spare" before I had a chance to buy another one . . .

I arrived in Glen Douglas just before it got dark, and found an excellent parking place – solid and level and, despite the rain, with a wonderful view in all directions – just a mile or so from the main Loch Lomond road. I sat in the Bongo, had a cup of tea and read a book until it got dark, then climbed into the back and played my guitar for a while until I reckoned it was late enough for me to go down to the pub just down the road without appearing to be too desperate for a drink.

I drove back down to the main road, pulled into the pub car park . . . and there was not a sign of life. It seemed that, although there was nothing to say as much, on Mondays the inn was closed.

I could of course have simply driven back to my parking place and rustled up a quick meal in the van, but by that time my heart – and stomach – was set on something more substantial, so, even though I didn't feel like driving much further in such dreadful weather, I headed south to the village of Luss (a favourite for coach tours because it's where a TV series called "Take The High Road" was filmed), where I knew there was at least one hotel which, surely, would be open.

It was the Loch Lomond Arms, an 18th century village inn which had quite recently been beautifully renovated into a modern, luxury hotel which deserved something rather better than the old clothes I wear on a typical Bongo Night.

A pint of Belhaven and a tasty plateful of haggis and neeps put me in contented mood, which I was happy to share with the couple on the adjacent table, who, like most people I met, loved the idea that they had played a part – albeit a very small one – in my Bongo Night adventures. They told me they lived in Walsall but came to Loch Lomond as often as they could because it was their favourite place on earth (I was tempted to suggest that if they were a bit more adventurous and went a few miles further north they would find even more beautiful scenery without the disadvantage of having to share it with hordes of TV-watching pensioners, but they were nice people so I kept my views to myself).

Not for the first time I awoke after a wet and windy night to find sunlight streaming through the windows of the Bongo. The demoralising bleakness of the night before had been replaced by a bright winter's morning, and the only sign of the rain was the huge puddle in which I found I was now parked. I noticed that the edges of the puddle were made jagged white with frost, the tarmac of the road was polished black and there was a hint of ice on the windscreen.

A few cars came very slowly up the hill and continued past me, their occupants presumably on their way to work at the Faslane nuclear submarine base just over the hill on Loch Fyne. And then a small van, labelled Luss Estates Management in elegant letters, pulled into my lay-by and parked just behind me.

I opened the door of the Bongo and climbed out, preparing myself for a telling-off. I could imagine that the owners of the Luss Estates might take a dim view of campervans being parked overnight on their land.

"Grand morning," he said with a smile. "But mind how you go, it's icier than you might think."

He was right. The ground was skimmed with a layer of almost invisible ice and my feet seemed to have developed a mind of their own as they struggled to keep me upright. So that was why the cars had been travelling so slowly.

"Blimey!" I said.

"Aye, it was a hard frost last night," the man said in a disconcerting Welsh accent. "Were you warm enough in there?"

I could see there was no need to pretend that I had not spent the night there, so assured him that the Bongo was a pretty snug little vehicle, and that once I'd got into bed I had no idea that the temperatures were plummeting outside.

He told me he envied me, being able to wake up in such a place on such a morning. "It's not always as good as this, mind – in fact it hardly ever is!"

He told me his job as a ranger with Luss Estates required him to come here every morning, to check for injured sheep or deer and to make sure all the fences and stone walls were still standing.

"It's not a bad job," he admitted.

I had arranged to meet May, my old friend from our days together at the Nottingham Evening Post, at about lunchtime in the Kelvingrove Museum in Glasgow so I was in no hurry to leave Glen Douglas. Even then I had time to continue on the road towards Faslane and Helensburgh, to enjoy the magnificent coastal road along Loch Fyne before heading back to the city.

I had wondered if I would recognise May, and even if I did whether we would have anything in common after so long.

But of course I recognised her; and of course she recognised me. While there was not much truth in our mutual claims that "You haven't changed a bit!", neither of us had changed so much that we no longer looked like the people we had been 30 years before.

This was another surprise of my Bongo Nights. I had already found that they were a good way of meeting some lovely, interesting new people . . . and now I was discovering they were an excellent way of rekindling old friendships too.

24
HONISTER
Cumbria
Friday December 12

From the early days of my Bongo Night adventure I had had one parking spot at the back of my mind which I knew would be perfectly magnificent on a night in the depths of the winter: A large, level site beside a huge boulder on the lower slopes of the Honister Pass in the Lake District, just where the valley opens up after the road descends dramatically in a series of tight bends and even steeper hills once it has come over the top from Borrowdale.

It was one of the places I had suggested to the young couple I met at the top of Newlands on Bongo Night No 3 and every time I had passed it since then (which was often, since it lies in one of my favourite parts of the Lake District) I had told myself: "One day I'll be spending the night there."

I knew precisely when I would want to be there, when I would want to wake up and pull open the curtains to see the magnificence beyond – a perfect frosty winter's morning, with the sun adding a soft golden glow to the snow on the felltops as it rose on the mountains behind me.

And if it happened to be so cold that there were little icebergs in the stream as it tumbled down the valley beside me . . . so much the better!

The weather forecasts in the third week of December told me I was never going to get a better chance. It would be bitterly cold, they said, and there would be snow on the tops, but the dawn would bring bright sunshine, with only an off-chance of a brief wintry shower. I needed no further invitation.

I arrived in the dark under a sky lit by thousands of stars, and despite the cold I got out of the Bongo, just to stand quietly, to enjoy the stillness and remoteness of such a place.

I slept well, but woke in the night, and left the Bongo for a few minutes to marvel at the scene in which I was such a small part – a scene by now illuminated by a full moon which showed me, for the first time, that there was indeed snow on the tops.

In the morning I cooked my breakfast (why does bacon and eggs always taste so much better in a place like that?) and spent more than an hour walking around my territory in the sunshine, investigating the stream, sitting on rocks . . . and simply enjoying being there.

A few cars passed in each direction, and their drivers mostly waved in friendly (and, I liked to think, envious) fashion when they saw me.

I was planning to continue in the direction I'd been heading the night before, going on to Buttermere and then up over Newlands to Keswick, but as I sat in the driver's seat about to start the engine I noticed that the mountains ahead of me had disappeared. Where Buttermere had been there was now a thick dirty white cloud (whether snow or fog I couldn't tell). I had no wish to drive into that, so – after making a quick mental calculation involving the speed that the cloud seemed to be heading towards me – I made a speedy three-point turn and headed back up the hill which I had come down just a few hours before.

Above me and ahead of me the sun was shining; behind me it was nearly dark.

I was nearly at the top of the hill, basking in the sunshine and congratulating myself on making such a wise decision, when I noticed

it was snowing. Just a little at first, a few flakes falling from an incongruously blue sky. Then a little more. Then much more. Then it went dark. And the few snowflakes turned into a blizzard. And almost before I knew it the Bongo was no longer climbing the hill; it was sliding backwards, back down the way I had come and out of control towards either a stone wall to my left or a sheer drop down into a ravine to my right. Skidding backwards down a steep hill in a two-ton campervan, the driver doesn't have much choice. He simply has to sit there and await developments. I vaguely remember shouting "Shit!" at the top of my voice, but otherwise could merely wait and see which way the laws of gravity would take me. Into the wall or over the cliff?
Fortunately they chose the wall.
The front of the van swung suddenly to the right, as if it had decided that there was just about room to do a 180 degree turn so it could drive sedately back to the bottom of the hill as if nothing had happened, but as it did so the rear hit the wall with a deep scrunch, leaving the Bongo stranded almost broadside across the road.
I got out . . . and nearly fell flat on my back. It's a cliché to say the road was like an ice rink, but the road was like an ice rink.
I could see that there were no other cars coming up the hill behind me, but of greater concern was what might come over the brow of the hill – and how fast – about 50 yards ahead of me.
Anyone coming towards me at anything other than snail's pace would be unable to stop in those conditions and would have no choice but to slither into the side of the stranded Bongo.
I headed on foot up the hill with great difficulty, slipping and falling and cursing and praying that I would be in time to flag down any approaching traffic.
The first car was driven by a mountain rescue volunteer on his way to a training exercise in the valley. The second was a brand new Land-Rover containing a film crew from London who were planning to spend the day making a promotional video advertising their vehicle's prowess on difficult terrain.
We all stood around the Bongo (most of us hanging onto wing mirrors, door handles and any other protuberances that might stop us sliding on our backsides down the hill) and quickly came to the

conclusion that there was nothing we could do,

The road was so slippery there was no hope of shifting the van with manpower alone, and the idea of the Land-Rover further demonstrating its capabilities by reversing back up the hill towing the Bongo as it went, was also soon ruled out.

The only hope was that the staff at the Honister Slate Mine at the top of the hill – who we knew were already out salting the other side so that any customers could make it up the drag from Keswick – would, when they'd finished, come down to us on our side and help us clear the road well enough for the Bongo's tyres to grip.

To say that I was embarrassed was putting it mildly! How many times had I sat at home in bad weather, listening to BBC Radio Cumbria reports that various passes in the Lake District were blocked – not by the snow, but by vehicles – campervans, even – which had proved incapable of getting through it?

And how many times had I harrumphed: "Stupid bloody idiots! They shouldn't have been there in these conditions in the first place."

The mountain rescue man was very sympathetic. "It's not your fault," he said. "The sun was shining when you started, so how were you to know? It could have happened to any of us. You were just unlucky."

The boss of the Slate Mine said more or less the same thing when he eventually came over the horizon in a digger tractor, with a young woman assistant cheerfully shovelling salt and sand from the bucket on the front.

They gingerly brought the digger to within a few feet of the Bongo (they didn't want it sliding down the hill any more than I did) and spread extra shovelfuls of salt under my wheels. We waited and watched for a few minutes while the salt did its job and the tarmac began to emerge from under the freshly fallen snow.

The digger trundled back to the top of the hill and the mountain rescue man looked at me.

"Go on, give it a try," he said. "If you get going, just keep going . . . and don't stop till you get to the top."

I started the engine and gently pressed the accelerator. The Bongo eased forwards and I cautiously turned the steering wheel to point it up the hill rather than towards the chasm.

The wheels gripped, the onlookers cheered . . . and I drove in stately style to the top of the hill.

In the Slate Mine's car park I thanked all those who'd helped – not just for their patience and their muscles, but the kind words with which they tried to convince me I was not to blame. Not my fault? I still think it was. I'm local and know enough to know the reputation of the Honister Pass, and to know that the weather conditions on it can change in a flash.

The whole episode lasted about two hours and it cost me a dent in the Bongo's tailgate, a badly bent rear bumper, £20 I put in the Slate Mine's charity box . . . and a whole lot of wounded pride.

25
PORT GLASGOW
Scotland
Wednesday December 17

In December my 94-year-old mother was taken to hospital after being found coughing up blood in the care home in which she lives just off the sea front at Weston-super-Mare. She was, by all accounts, nearly dead when she arrived at the hospital, but after a few blood transfusions – by which time Tricia and I had rushed down the motorway to (as we thought) say goodbye to her – she was back to her perky, spiky self.

As we walked into her ward at Weston-super-Mare General Hospital, she was bright-eyed and sitting up in bed.

"You're late," she said as she saw us walking through the door.

Hopes that she had quickly recovered from whatever it was that she had had been suffering from were proved a little premature though, and a week or so after our visit I had another call from my sister, who lives in Weston too, warning that perhaps I ought to visit her again because she seemed to be fading once more.

Tricia could not come with me this time, and the idea of another 600-mile round trip down the motorway on my own in the middle of winter held no appeal at all, so – remembering how easy it had been taking Mel to Glasgow airport – I decided to fly down instead. There was a plane down to Bristol at 7am and another back at 8pm, so it would be possible to do the whole trip in just one day if I found somewhere to spend a Bongo Night fairly near the airport.

My chosen spot was just a 20-minute drive from the airport, in a lay-by on the hills above Port Glasgow, looking down on the River Clyde.

When I arrived it was teeming with rain, but that only made the twinkling lights below an even more magical sight. There I was in a quiet, secluded spot – reached by a quite hairy drive along some narrow country lanes that led through an area of unspoiled moorland – and I was looking down on the floodlit factories and oil depots that lined the busy dual carriageway that led into one of Britain's greatest cities.

And when the rain eased off I could make out the black shape of the Clyde, with still more twinkling lights on the other side.

I could only imagine what the view would have been like in a past age, when the Clyde was a flourishing port and the centre of Britain's shipbuilding industry, and when mighty ships like the Lusitania, the Queen Mary and the QE2 would have been sailing down the river beneath me.

I only have to see a river like the Clyde – or the Avon of my childhood near Bristol – to feel a great sadness at the decline of Britain's maritime industries, if not the decline of Britain itself. How wonderful these places used to be, how bustling and thriving and energetic they were, and how tired and dispirited they seem now.

It was the wettest, wildest, windiest night I had experienced yet on my Bongo travels, and the van was rocking wildly as if it was a ship on the high seas, which just added to the nautical flavour of my dreams. I went to sleep remembering the thrills I used to get seeing great ships – no, any ships, even the humble little coasters that plied the Bristol Channel when I was a child – and regretting that the age of watching them from viewpoints such as this had gone.

My alarm woke me at six, I was on the move within 15 minutes and pulling into the airport car park less than half an hour after that.

By 11 o'clock I was sitting beside my Mum's bed in hospital, marvelling at how an old lady who just the day before had seemed so sick could be quite as sparkly-eyed and ruddy-cheeked as she was now.

    I caught the evening plane to Glasgow – and was back home before midnight – confident that this time Mum really was over the worst. And I was right. When she was discharged about a fortnight later the only lasting effect of her illness was that in her time in hospital she had forgotten how to send messages on the mobile phone she calls her "text machine"..

26
SUNBIGGIN TARN
Cumbria
Tuesday December 30

More than 20 years ago Tricia and I completed the Coast To Coast Walk – 192 miles across the north of England, from St Bees in Cumbria to Robin Hood's Bay in Yorkshire. It was the first time I had ever attempted, let alone accomplished, such a feat of physical endurance and the sense of achievement afterwards was extraordinary – so extraordinary that when I returned to work on the next Monday morning, only to discover that the managing director had taken advantage of my absence to engineer my sacking, I looked upon my unexpected unemployment as little more than a minor hiccup on the journey of my life.

If I could manage a walk like that, I reckoned, I could manage whatever life threw at me, even if it included not having a job.

My favourite part of the walk was not the trek over the magnificent Lake District fells, nor the lonely beauty of the York Moors, nor even the final few miles alongside the North Sea . . . it was the short stretch through the gentler farmland of East Cumbria, past the rocky limestone outcrops around Orton and onto the lovely little Sunbiggin Tarn. It was to Sunbiggin Tarn that I returned for my 25th Bongo Night on December 30 – a few days late because I had not been able to get away over Christmas.

It was a filthy evening, and I confess my heart was not really in it, so I set off late after making up the bed in the Bongo, so that when I arrived I could simply climb into the back, go to sleep and hope for something better in the morning.

Sunbiggin is only about 30 miles from home, and most of the journey could be done by motorway. But I had plenty of time, and I didn't fancy fighting against the teeming rain on the M6, so I took lesser roads instead.

However, motorway or no, the route still had to take me close to Shap summit – which at 916ft above sea level can provide some of the worst driving conditions in Britain – and it was there that I Iencountered such a thick bank of fog that I could see barely 20 yards ahead of me. Visibility on the motorway would have been just as bad, it's true, but there the road would have been more or less straight, while on my B-road I had to contend with a series of downhill bends with the edges almost impossible to pick out in the Bongo's notoriously poor headlights.The fog began to clear just as I saw the first signpost to Sunbiggin Tarn, but I waited at a junction to let a Mondeo go ahead of me, on the assumption that he was probably local and therefore knew the road. I used him as a guide as the road cut through scenery which, even in the dark, I could see was becoming steadily more wild . . . then suddenly we were there. I recognised the path down which we had walked all those years before, then picked out the dark mass of the tarn on my right, spotted the lay-by in which I would be spending the night . . . and watched as the Mondeo pulled into it.

I could, of course, have pulled in immediately behind him, but I reckoned that might be misconstrued as a threat or (remembering my experience in the dogging lay-by on the way to Sheffield) something worse, so I continued for about a mile, to the top of a hill where I knew there was another acceptable, though not quite as attractive, wildcamping place.

I did a quick three-point turn to pull into it, and as I turned off the engine I saw the tail lights of a car disappearing down the valley along the road which I – and the Mondeo – had just come up. Since the Mondeo and I were the only vehicles on the road that night, it was a pretty safe bet that he had merely pulled into the lay-by, maybe had a cigarette or a very quick snog with his girlfriend, before turning round and heading back whence he had come. I started the engine, drove back to the tarn and parked in the newly vacated lay-by just as I had intended.

In the morning a few cars passed before I got up (presumably people commuting to places like Penrith or Carlisle from their homes in the villages further up the valley), and later I spotted a woman walking her dog from a car parked further down the road. But apart from them I had the place to myself.

When I opened the curtains I could see the sun was beginning to rise above the fells on my left, and soon everywhere was bathed in an extraordinary pinkness, which lit up the sky, the hills and the lake as if it was the garishly painted scenery in a pantomime.

I had originally planned to cook my breakfast there, but I had woken in the night, remembering that I was not many miles from the Westmorland Services on the motorway at Tebay, where could be had one of the finest cooked breakfasts in the country. Why waste time and effort cooking bacon, egg, mushrooms and fried bread in the cramped space of the Bongo when, for just a few pounds, I could get the same – only better – just up the road.

Instead I just had a cup of coffee and a banana, before setting off to do the one thing I wanted to do before I left.

It was a weird, wonderful, perfect day for an early morning walk (and anyway I wanted to get a photograph of the Bongo from the far side of the tarn) so I put on my wellies and headed off across the soggy marshland that lay between me and the higher ground in the distance.

It was a tough walk – there is no distinct path, and the only way of getting there is to splodge through the reeds around the lake before emerging onto something slightly more solid on the other side – but there is something magical about being able to fall out of bed into a wonderful location like that.

I knew there was no other way I would have been walking in such a place so early in the morning. If I had been at home I would probably have still been in bed, ignorant of the lovely day that was dawning on the other side of the still-drawn curtains.

So not for the first time in my Bongo adventures, I thought: It's mornings like this that make it all worthwhile.

27
TROUTBECK
Cumbria
Wednesday December 31

The beautiful day did not last long, and I was soon reminded that a red sky in the morning truly is a shepherd's warning – particularly for any shepherds who don't much enjoy monsoon rain being blown into their faces by gale force winds. That's what I experienced a couple of hours later when I arrived for my next Bongo Night stop, at the Camping and Caravan Club's site at Troutbeck, between Penrith and Keswick, a mere 20 miles in distance (but a world away in weather) from Sunbiggin Tarn.

For many years, ever since we stopped having New Year parties at our house and none of our friends stepped in to host them instead, Tricia and I have liked to do something a bit different on New Year's Eve. We have had late-night picnics in the Lake District, lit a bonfire on top of the hill in our garden, parked in lofty lay-bys to watch the midnight fireworks of towns below us, and run a tournament in our greenhouse which is big enough to hold a full sized table tennis table.

The idea this year (fuelled by my 52-week Bongo Night adventure) was to meet with friends – the same friends with whom we had camped before my bizarre experience in Morecambe Bay – who had their own campervans, and celebrate the start of 2015 together.

The rest of the party did not share my enthusiasm for camping in the wild (Tricia is not the only one who appreciates her toilets) so, after finding that all of our first choices were already fully booked – it's surprising how many campervanners and caravanners are, like us, daft enough to want to go away in the middle of winter – we settled on Troutbeck.

In truth it seemed a pretty good choice. It was not very far from home, had all the facilities we might need and, best of all, had magnificent views of the Lake District mountains and was handily placed so that at midnight we would be able to enjoy the fireworks with which the people of Keswick chose to celebrate the New Year.

I had imagined what it would be like, meeting Tricia and our friends and seeing in the New Year in such a beautifully scenic place, but whatever I had imagined it wasn't this.

I had driven there straight from Sunbiggin Tarn and expected to be able to await Tricia's arrival by taking a gentle stroll along the nearby lanes, passing the time by taking evocative photographs or painting a watercolour of the view. But only a fool would have left his campervan voluntarily in such weather, and though I knew the Lake District mountains were there somewhere, I just could not see them. Indeed it was raining so hard I could barely see beyond the caravan site's perimeter fence.

It was raining when I arrived soon after noon. It was raining when my friend Betty arrived a couple of hours later with Tricia in the passenger seat of her smart VW van and it was raining when Val and Albert arrived in their splendid motorhome just before it got dark (or even darker than it had been for most of the day).

We parked side by side in our allotted pitches, facing west towards Keswick and the fells that surround it but we could have been parked in the flat lands of East Anglia for all that we could see.

There was nothing for it but to start our New Year celebrations early, so by five o'clock the five of us had gathered in Albert's van for afternoon tea, and that was quickly followed by something alcoholic, which – though I favoured leaving the food till later on the grounds that we would need something to do to break up the long hours waiting for midnight – in turn soon gave way to olives and oatcakes, a thick beef stew (which I had cooked at home the previous day and reheated in the Bongo that afternoon) and an excellent lemon and raspberry pudding baked by Betty.

We had started looking at our watches early on ("Only six and a half hours to go") and were still looking at them ("Only four hours now") when we finished our meal.

It was all great fun – our mood helped, without doubt, by the absurdity of it all – but what on earth do five people do in a campervan when it's raining so hard only an idiot would poke his nose outside?

I fetched my guitar from the Bongo (something I had not intended to do – but I reckoned we just had to have something apart from alcohol to pass the time): "Only two and a half now."

And we had some more olives: "Only one and a half."

And cake: "Only 40 minutes – I think we're going to make it."

We turned on the radio and listened to the chimes of Big Ben (which on Radio 4 followed, rather inappropriately, I thought, a discussion on assisted suicide) and, with some relief, wished each other a happy new year.

I threw open the door of the campervan and, even though it was still raining, went outside to watch the fireworks.

I could still see no further than the fence. But if I listened very carefully I could just about hear the swoosh and boom of the rockets over Keswick.

28
WATENDLATH
Cumbria
Wednesday January 7

When Visit Britain – the part of the British Tourist Authority whose job it is to "market Britain to the rest of the world" – chose to promote Wales with a photograph of the English Lake District my fate was set.

I was watching the local BBC news when my TV reporter friend Alison (who, you might remember, had an old VW campervan which failed to make the journey to meet us for Bongo Night 10) came on screen to tell us that "a mistake" had led the tourist board to use the picture of Ashness Bridge above Derwentwater in Cumbria, England, as an illustration of what visitors might find awaiting them in the Brecon Beacons, 250 miles away in Powys, Wales.

Seeing the film of Alison walking at Ashness Bridge, with the lake and the fells of Skiddaw and Whinlatter behind her, I realised that here was a perfect place for a Bongo Night. I knew it quite well, and was surprised I had not thought of it before.

There were several parking spots which would provide a safe, secluded and level place to spend the night and – best of all – I liked the idea of going to a place within 40 miles of home which some unthinking bureaucrat in London had just accidentally and inexplicably transplanted to Wales.

The forecast was for dire weather all week – heavy rain on most days, gale force winds on some, and both on a few – so I settled on the night which seemed to offer the best chance of my awaking to sunshine (pulling back the curtains after a good night's sleep and looking out upon some wonderful scenery bathed by the morning sun is one of the very best aspects of Bongoing).

I spent the evening in Keswick – enjoying another excellent goulash in the Dog and Gun, before walking in the rain to the cinema to see "The Theory of Everything" – so it was gone 10pm when I set out off down the road beside Derwentwater, splashing through the puddles towards Borrowdale and the Honister Pass before diving to the left and climbing the hill on the little road which leads ever more steeply up the fell until eventually it peters out altogether in the tiny hamlet of Watendlath.

I passed Ashness Bridge and the car park beside it, and continued further up the hill, until the trees thinned out at the place known as Surprise View from where I knew that in the morning I would – cloud and rain permitting – be able to enjoy one of the finest panoramas in Britain.

There are a couple of small car parks here and I chose the lower one, purely because that was the first I caught in my headlights.

As I pulled to a stop I noted to my relief that the site was perfectly level, so I was able simply to park without much thought before turning off the engine, opening the door and stepping out . . . straight into a puddle. The car park was, I discovered on closer inspection, liberally dotted with large muddy puddles (which would become deeper and muddier as the night progressed) and I managed to tread in a couple more as I walked a few paces for a pee in the dark.

The night was wild and wet, with the Bongo rocking in the ever increasing wind and me wondering how wise it was to park, in those conditions, beneath so many trees, any one of which might have come crashing down on the Bongo at any moment. It was not a good night for sleeping!

But by the morning the rain had stopped, the wind had subsided just a little and – as I found when I peeped through the curtain – the light from the rising sun was beginning to pick out the tops of the highest mountains on the far side of the lake.

The view across the lake towards Whinlatter was as beautiful as I'd hoped, and I enjoyed it to the full, leaving the delicious smell of the cooking bacon to follow me as I wandered over to take the inevitable photographs. But this was not really why I was here – it wasn't quite the spot which Visit Britain had claimed to be Welsh.

So after breakfast I packed up the van and drove a mile or so back down the hill to the car park adjacent to Ashness Bridge, so I could take my own version of the iconic photograph which the tourist board had used in its bizarre claim that, despite all appearances, I was in fact in Wales.

I walked to the bridge, and spotted a rock on the far side of the river which seemed to offer the best vantage point. It was a tricky manoeuvre – particularly on rocks so wet from the overnight rain – but I managed it, and took the photograph without incident. It was only on my way back to the Bongo, as I made my way across a small patch of grass which nestled among the rocks, that things went dramatically wrong.

My right foot shot forward on the wet grass, and my left followed it. I crashed onto my back, somehow avoiding any of the rocks that could have caused me even more serious injury, and I screamed from an agonising pain in my ankle. I dragged myself to a sitting position, then cautiously clambered to my feet, only to fall down again when my leg refused to take my weight. A sprain, I thought, and probably a bad one.

I hobbled back to the Bongo, yelping with pain and cursing myself for being so careless as to slip on a piece of grass when I'd successfully negotiated so many things that were so much more dangerous. But at least it was my left leg that I'd hurt – the leg a driver doesn't need when driving an automatic like the Bongo.

When I got home (my arrival delayed by a painful bit of shopping in the Booths supermarket in Keswick) I decided to seek the opinion of my GP to confirm my view that I had suffered nothing worse than a sprain. It took him only two minutes to examine my leg, pull a face and tell me I needed to go to hospital for an X-ray.

An hour later, after a surprisingly speedy passage through the A&E department at the Cumberland Infirmary in Carlisle, I knew the worst: I had broken my leg, low down towards my left ankle, and would need a temporary plastercast until the next day when an orthopaedic consultant would examine it further.

The idea of having a broken leg did not bother me overmuch. Plenty of people suffer much worse and carry on with their lives easily enough. What really worried me was how I was going to manage to keep my Bongo Night challenge going.

How could I possibly manage 24 more Bongo Nights if for the next six weeks my leg was going to be encased in plaster?

29
HOW MILL
Cumbria
Saturday January 17

In fact, though my leg was broken, it was not a particularly bad break. I had broken the fibula (the small bone that runs down the side of the leg) but had contrived to do it in a way which had not actually moved or dislodged it. So once the temporary plastercast was taken off, I was given instead a "moon boot" – a much more convenient contraption, which allowed me greater movement in greater comfort than I was expecting.

Even so, I had no idea whether I would be able to manage a night in the Bongo with a broken leg. Tricia had told me she would come with me, and drive me to wherever I wanted to go, but that was only part of it. Would I be able to move about well enough? To go to bed? To get out if I needed a pee in the night? Would I even be able to get into the van at all?

The only way of finding out was to try. So I did. Bongo Night number 29 was spent in the van parked outside our house.

We are lucky. We have a huge garden, and there is a big parking area – big enough for half a dozen campervans – at the top of our bumpy old drive, with a level concrete area just outside the front door. So it was an obvious place for me to find out whether I could continue with my Bongo Night adventure or do the sensible thing and take a break for a while.

It went well. I managed to climb into the van, managed to make the bed, managed to sleep like a log and – next morning – managed to cook breakfast for Tricia before she went out for a day's walking with her friends.

And somehow the fact that it had snowed overnight, and left the garden and the Bongo looking particularly lovely under a thick white cloak, simply emphasised my belief that my Bongo Nights, come what may, and with just a little adjustment to take account of a broken leg and two crutches, could and would continue.

30
WATERMILLOCK
Ullswater, Cumbria
Thursday January 22

My favourite of all the Lake District lakes is Ullswater. Not just because it is the closest to home, though that does help, but also because it has the most beautiful scenery, the best walks which don't leave you knackered for a week afterwards, and the best boats (Ullswater steamers look and feel like the real thing, unlike those on Derwentwater and, to a lesser extent, Windermere which are glorified taxis). And, in the Brackenrigg Inn overlooking the lake from the shore at Watermillock, it has one of the best pubs.

We first stayed at the Brackenrigg years before we ever thought of moving to Cumbria, have stayed there a couple of times since, and now regularly go there for meals and/or drinks. It is one of those pubs which, despite a frequent turnover of staff, always seem to manage to employ people who are efficient and friendly. And for several years now the food has been a notch or two above that which is served at most establishments in the Lake District.

It is also one of Tricia's favourites, which – since it was the first on which I was using her as my driver while I was incapacitated with my broken leg – was good enough reason to call in there on Bongo Night Number 30.

Our intention was to have a meal at the Brackenrigg before driving a few more miles down the lake to a lay-by which I know is often frequented by campervans in high summer, but which was unlikely to be so in the middle of winter. The lay-by would be a great place in which to wake up. Pulling back the curtain to see that familiar view down my favourite lake with Hallin Fell and the hills of High Street on the other side, would be a memorable and, since it was only 25 miles from home, easily achieved treat.

As so often, my intention came to nothing. A wonderful meal, nice local beer, a blazing log fire, friendly staff . . . it was all too much.

"Would you like anything else?" the barman asked. "Another drink?"

"That," I told him, "depends. How would you feel if we asked to sleep in our campervan in your car park?"

"Absolutely no problem at all," he said. "People do it all the time."

"In that case I'll have a whisky," I said.

And Tricia, who had initially shaken her head in refusal, worried about drink-driving on the short distance to our chosen lay-by, said: "I'll have a hot chocolate with courvoisier, please."

We were the last ones to leave the bar – and we did that only after establishing that if we presented ourselves for breakfast at about 8.30 the staff would be glad to serve us that as well.

We woke up the next morning with a view of Ullswater – not the view I'd promised myself but a pretty decent one nonetheless, with a slate grey lake and an angry dark sky emphasising the whiteness of the snow on the far fells.

And I didn't have to cook breakfast.

31
NEWCASTLETON
Scottish Borders
Sunday January 25

The 31st of my 52 Bongo Nights was special because it was something Tricia and I had been planning for many weeks, ever since we'd seen that the Dubliners (or what remains of them) would be playing at the Buccleuch Centre, an unlikely little theatre in the small town of Langholm in the Scottish Borders.

It was a good chance to combine a night out – Irish music had become special to us, thanks to our trips to Donegal – with a Bongo Night in one of my favourite places for peaceful wild camping and, though I had not visualised doing it with a broken leg, it was one I was very much looking forward to. Neither of us expected the evening to begin with a pool of blood . . .

The Buccleuch Centre is a welcoming little place – a purpose-built theatre, complete with auditorium, restaurant and bar, all staffed by volunteers – and Langholm is a welcoming little town, so it came as a surprise to find a red sticky trail on the floor when we arrived.

The blood lay thick and deeply red in little puddles, all the way from the entrance foyer to the bar, and people were beginning to tiptoe around it, careful not to get it on the soles of their shoes. The trail led clearly to an elderly man, who was holding a glass of wine, engaged in busy conversation with a group of friends and – until a stranger tapped him on his shoulder – totally unaware that blood was pouring from the bottom of his trousers.

He and his three friends were gently led away by one of the volunteers, while others searched the place for something to wipe the floor with – a more difficult challenge than you might expect, since no one could find a mop until most of the job had been done by liberal use of paper towels.

We guessed that the unfortunate man had unknowingly gashed his leg on his car door as he arrived outside the theatre, but whatever the cause he played no further part in the evening, which left me as probably the most incapacitated member of the audience.

It was only after beginning my climb up the steps to my seat that I realised that, living in a bungalow, I had no idea how to manage stairs on crutches. It is, I discovered, one thing using crutches along the flat and quite another using them to climb a staircase, albeit a small one. And the more I concentrated, the more I tried to work out how best to do it, the more difficult it became (a lack of co-ordination confirmed during the interval, when – with the unintended result of providing entertainment for a theatre full of captivated spectators – I found going downstairs to the loo even more difficult than going up).

After the show Tricia drove the Bongo out of Langholm, up the hill, past the spot where, 20 weeks before, I had parked in my failed attempt to see the Northern Lights, and out along the spectacularly beautiful road towards Newcastleton. It seems that visibility is in short supply in that vicinity, for just as I had not been able to see more than a few yards when hoping to see the aurora, Tricia could not see more than a few yards when trying to make out the road ahead of her. The visibility was lost in great rolling blankets of low cloud, which with the Bongo's less than perfect headlights made it impossible to spot potential parking places until we had passed them, but suddenly the murk cleared just in time for us to see a big parking space a little way beyond the smaller pull-in alongside a cattle grid.

Tricia manoeuvred the van so that we knew it was facing outwards (though the chances of our needing a quick getaway seemed remote indeed), but in truth it was too foggy for us to tell what sort of place we had parked in. And for now it didn't matter anyway, because we simply climbed into the back and fell asleep.

I did wake briefly, to hear the sound of rain gently beating on the roof – long enough to wonder if in fact it was snow, and ask myself what we would do if we found ourselves marooned under three feet of it when we looked out in the morning. In such an isolated spot, with no houses within sight, no mobile signal, no passing traffic and, with my broken leg, no hope of walking anywhere to get help, we would simply have to stay in the Bongo until it melted, no matter how long that might be. The prospect didn't alarm me. We were in a campervan, after all, and we had a cupboard full of supplies to keep us from starvation for several days.

When dawn broke there was no sign of snow. Just a rather damp and very windy Scottish morning, with a faint hint of sunshine (or at least brightness) low in the sky to the east.

We could see now, for the first time, just where we had spent the night – on top of the moors, with mile after mile of nothingness in each direction. Grouse were calling in the distance, but otherwise there was not a sound.

This was the way the best Bongo Nights were supposed to end, I thought. A world away from anywhere, with fantastic views in all directions. I was glad Tricia was with me, because it would show her – if she needed showing – what it was about my Bongo adventure that made it so worthwhile.

32
DRUMBURN
Near Dumfries, Scotland
Friday February 13

When I went back to the hospital for a check-up a month after breaking my leg I was confident that the doctor would tell me I was doing so well I could now dispense with my crutches, wear my moonboot some of the time, but not all of it, and generally start getting on with my life again. I could, after all, stand up, walk and wriggle my toes (all more or less unaided, and without very much pain) so in my mind there was nothing to stop me sitting in the driving seat and resuming my Bongo travels. I had even decided where I would be driving myself – to the Scottish coast, that very night – to celebrate my newly regained freedom.

I was wrong.

The doctor told me that broken bones take six weeks to mend, not just four, and the fact that my leg hurt at all was a sign that I was not yet ready to resume a normal life.

"How about driving?" I asked, though I already knew what his answer would be. "I've got an automatic, so I don't really need my left leg."

He shook his head, but grinned at my keenness to put an end to my infirmity.

"You would almost certainly be all right," he said. "Almost – but it's not a risk worth taking. Give it another couple of weeks or so."

Tricia, on hearing the news, was typically upbeat.

"You can still go tonight – I'll come with you."

We returned home from the hospital, making plans to load up the Bongo and head straight off to Glen Caple, near Dumfries, where after my second Bongo Night I had bumped into Judge Batty in the welcoming car park overlooking the little harbour.

We had temporarily forgotten about the thin layer of icy snow that had been lying on our drive for several days.

But when we got home there it was in front of us, an unavoidable reminder that, though our all-wheel drive Subaru could cope with such conditions with ease, the Bongo could not.

"We'd never get down the drive – not in the Bongo," she said. "Remember Honister!"

I didn't need reminding of my frightening slide backwards downhill just a few weeks before, so I knew she was right.

"We'd be asking for trouble," I agreed.

That night we both slept in our bed, in our house.

A week later the snow had gone and I had enough confidence in my leg to have dispensed with the moonboot for most of the day. It was, after all, only a few days less than six weeks since I had broken it . . . long enough, as the doctor had told me, for the bone to be properly healed. And anyway I was getting sick of being stuck at home – and I knew that Tricia would not be there much to keep me company and stop me getting more and more miserable.

She would, as usual, be spending her Friday evening at the climbing wall, and for most of the next day – February 14th – she would be walking in the Lake District with her ladies' fellwalking group.

I knew I had two choices: Stay at home alone, becoming ever more angry at whoever it was who had organised the walks calendar so that it took women away from their partners on St Valentine's Day (someone who clearly would not recognise romance if it got into bed with her, I thought) or go off and do something exciting on my own.

I packed the Bongo and as Tricia set off for her climbing evening I headed off for the Scottish coast – taking with me the Valentine's card she had left for me to open when the big day dawned,

At about ten o'clock – in pitch dark and hammering rain – I pulled into the "viewpoint" overlooking the Solway at Drumburn, a few miles west of the pretty village of New Abbey. This is a small car park, big enough for maybe four cars beside the road, but with space for three more on an elevated section which, if conditions are right, affords splendid views over the estuary and across to the Cumbrian coast and the Lake District mountains on the other side.

I could only hope that the weather forecasters had got it right when they said that no matter how bad things might be overnight I would wake up to blue skies and sunshine.

They had. When I pulled open the curtains in the morning I was greeted by the sun rising from behind the hills, splashing bright jewels of light across the high tide. Of all the sunrises I had seen on my Bongo Nights this was the most dramatic and I sat in the van for an hour watching as the sun lifted itself off the horizon in a colourful palette of silvers, golds and yellows. The only drawback was that it was so bright I could not see the Lake District mountains!

I eventually dragged myself away from Drumburn, and drove the short distance over the hills to Kippford, an attractive village, full of boats and tourists, set beside the River Urr shortly before it flows out into the Solway.

In the summer I would have struggled to find somewhere to park, but this was mid February and I was spoiled for choice. I pulled into the space nearest the slipway, grabbed my fleece . . . and went for a walk. Yes, a walk!

It was only a short walk, it's true – maybe 100 metres there, and 100 metres back – and I did it at a snail's pace. But I was walking. Properly walking, without crutches, without moonboot and without pain.

The pleasure was immense. I wanted to skip with joy, but realised that skipping with joy might not be such a good idea, so instead I simply smiled quietly to myself and resisted the temptation to shout at all the old ladies I met walking their dogs: "Look, I can walk!"

33
GRASMERE
Cumbria
Wednesday February 18

The weather forecast was still dreadful but since I had never before allowed the threat of heavy rain and gale-force winds to put me off I set off for the Lake District . . . just making a small concession that I would spend the night in a pub car park rather in some isolated spot high up on the fells.

I aimed for the Travellers Rest, at the bottom of Dunmail Raise near Grasmere (one of the tourist-packed 'honeypot' villages I usually make a point of avoiding). I knew it was a pleasant pub, and that they served good food and some of my favourite local beers, and I had a pretty good idea they allowed campervan-owning customers to spend the night in their good sized car park.

I asked for a pint of Cocker Hoop and, as I expected, the barmaid asked if I'd also like to see the menu.

"I'm not sure," I replied, as if the thought had only just occurred to me. "I've got a campervan. Would it be all right if I spent the night in it in your car park?"

I wanted to give the impression that if it wouldn't, I would have no option but to down my pint and head off for some other establishment where it would.

"Yes, that would be fine," she smiled. "And thank you for asking. Not everyone does."

She told me that the previous weekend five campervans had established themselves for three nights in the car park and nobody had bothered to ask for permission.

The barmaid was clearly still angry about it.

"They just left them there and went walking, taking the spaces we needed for other customers," she said. "And when they came back they hardly spent anything in here either. We weren't happy."

"I'm not surprised," I said. "That's just plain bad manners. And it gets the rest of us a bad name too!"

There wasn't a spare table in the main bar, so I took my pint up a couple of steps into an annex, where there were a few more tables and – further on – a couple of leather sofas and a log fire in an area marked off by a rope and labelled "For residents only".

A balding middle-aged man was sitting alone, nursing a pint at one of the tables, so I settled down at one of the others to await the lamb shank and mustard mash that I'd ordered.

Two lone men, in a dark corner of the pub, away from the hubbub of the busy bar next door . . .

"I hope you don't mind me disturbing you," I said, pulling a book from my pocket to show that he did not have to engage in conversation if he didn't want to.

"It's all right, I'm just going," he said, swallowing his remaining half pint of beer in little more than one gulp.

"I hope it wasn't something I said."

"No," he said, lifting his empty glass in my direction. "It's a bad habit to get into."

I wasn't sure quite what bad habit it was that he – or I – was in danger of getting into.

But then I noticed that I had chosen a table immediately next to the door to the gents.

Two lone men, in a dark corner of the pub, away from the hubbub of the busy bar next door and next to the door to the toilet, . . .

Surely he didn't think . . . Did he . . .?

I went back to the bar and bought a second pint, if only so I could continue my chat with the barmaid and show my new "friend" (if he was still there) that there was a perfectly good explanation for my being in a pub on my own.

And if I could get a mention of my wife, my three children and my two grandchildren into the conversation so much the better.

Maybe I was imagining the man's reaction to my joining him in that dingy corner, but even if I was it was enough to put me on my guard against any further possible misunderstandings.

So later on – at that stage of the evening when the staff come out from behind the bar and sit in a jovial huddle beside the fire – I thought it best not to go out to make my Bongo bed before returning for a whisky nightcap.

A man saying "I'm just off to make my bed" was the sort of thing that could be easily misinterpreted by an attractive barmaid at the end of a busy evening.

So I decided against the whisky, took my empty beer glass back to the bar, thanked the barmaid for her kindness and disappeared into the storm of the night.

And what a night it was! I tried watching a DVD on my laptop, but the rain beating on the roof of the Bongo made it impossible to hear most of the dialogue, and when I gave up and went to bed I could not sleep for the rocking of the van in the wind.

How thankful I was that I was in the relative shelter of the Travellers Rest car park and not in the full face of the gale in a lay-by on top of some mountain road.

34
ULLSWATER
Cumbria
Friday February 20

Two days later I was on the road again, making up for the week I had missed when the snow had stopped me getting out of my drive. Not that we had totally escaped the snow, though . . .

I had planned to spend this Bongo Night high up in the Pennine hills, deep into the wilderness land that lies on the Cumbria-County Durham border, beyond Alston, the picturesque little cobbled town which, at 1,000 ft above sea level boasts of being the highest market town in England.

But since the weather forecast warned of snow on high land – and land doesn't come much higher than the place I had intended to head for – I had to think again. The memory of my slide down the Honister pass was still vivid enough to deter me from taking any sort of chance with winter conditions.

The trouble was my second choice wasn't much better – a truly wild wildcamping spot, among the maze of minor roads in the hills near Shap (a place notorious among drivers as the most likely place for the

M6 motorway to be blocked by snow, gales or both).

Since I had no wish to be stranded there or anywhere else (especially as there would almost certainly be no mobile phone signal there, so I would not be able to call for help if the worst happened) the answer had to be Ullswater. This, as I have said several times before, is my favourite of the Lake District lakes (although pedants will tell you it is not a lake at all, since the only lake is Bassenthwaite, and all the others are meres, waters or tarns) and it is notable for the number of fine potential Bongo spots on both its east and west shores.

It is also exceptionally beautiful, comparatively quiet and undiscovered by the tourist masses . . . and my younger son Will, who works on the 'steamers' that ply their trade along its length, lives just three miles away from it.

My hastily rearranged evening was beginning to take shape – a leisurely drive down to the Lakes, a pint and a meal in the pub with Will, then a few miles further up the lake to the lay-by where I planned to spend the night.

The lay-by, when I got there, was so dark I could see nothing apart from what was illuminated by my headlights. Ullswater is not officially designated as a "dark sky" area, but that night it might as well have been. True, there was a faint glow from Penrith to the north-west, and the twinkling lights of a couple of houses on the far shore, but nothing could take away from the miracle of the thousands of stars overhead.

There was no sound apart from the gentle slurping of the lake as its waves kissed the little beach.

Not for the first time I thought how lucky I was to have Ullswater just down the road from home!

35
KESWICK
Cumbria
Thursday February 26

On the bleak winter days of February, when the weather forecasters speak of heavy rain, strong winds and plunging temperatures, there is not much incentive for a man to jump into his campervan for a trip to some sweet spot on the far side of the country. So my next trip was another short one – back down to Keswick for a night at the Castlerigg stone circle, the dramatic Neolithic monument which sits on a hill above the town, and offers panoramic views with the mountains of Helvellyn and High Seat as a backdrop.

There were several reasons for this choice, but the main one was that Castlerigg was a place where I had long wanted to spend the night. It being less than 40 miles from home, and the northern part of the Lake District that afternoon being bathed in unlikely sunshine . . . and Keswick's wonderful old cinema that evening showing a film I wanted to see, were others.

I timed it so that I arrived at Castlerigg just before sunset, simply because I reckoned that watching the sun go down would be a pretty special experience in a place which has been variously described as "perhaps the most atmospheric and dramatically sited of all British stone circles" and "one of the most visually impressive prehistoric monuments in Britain".

I was not the only one with that idea. A middle aged couple were already there – he setting up his camera on a tripod, ready for the classic shot of the stones being picked out in red as the sun set over Helvellyn in the distance, and she wandering moodily, hands shoved into her deepest pockets and blowing out her cheeks as the winter chill seeped into her bones (I got the feeling they had been there, waiting for the perfect photo opportunity, for some time).

"Just shout at me if I get in your way," I told him, knowing from experience how infuriating it can be when, just as the sun sinks into position behind the stones, some stranger walks into the shot you've been waiting more than half an hour for.

Later on, as he packed up his camera and folded away his tripod, he told me that he came from York, though, like me, he had been born in Devon. He too had a campervan, which he used often (Cumbria was his favourite place) but he had never thought of tackling anything like my 52-week Bongo challenge, even though his wife had marked the year after her 50th birthday by climbing 50 of the Lake District peaks.

I stayed until darkness fell and I could no longer see the silhouette of the distant mountains then drove down to the (relatively) bright lights of Keswick, where I just had time for a goulash (my third of these Bongo travels) in the Dog and Gun before making my way to the Alhambra, the cinema just up the road, for a screening of a film about Rembrandt.

The Alhambra had, during the course of these Bongo Nights, become my favourite ever cinema – and not just because it had provided a warm haven on my winter trips to the Lake District, when there was really not much to do in a small campervan.

It's a little gem, opened in 1913, and is now – thanks to its former manager Tom Rennie, who bought it when it was threatened with closure three years ago – one of the oldest continuously functioning cinemas in the country.

It is wonderfully quirky place which, though it is equipped with digital technology and satellite receiving equipment and shows films as up-to-date as anywhere in the country, also manages to transport its audiences back to the golden age more than 50 years before. As likely as not it will be Tom who sells you your ticket (a suitably old fashioned piece of cardboard, dispensed from a machine not unlike the contraption used by conductors on the buses of my childhood) and who, if you don't go for one of his tubs of Lakeland ice cream, suggests you might like to help yourself to a free coffee while you're waiting for the film to start.

You can choose between the stalls (£4.50 if you're an old folk like me) or £5.50 for those who choose a bit more luxury in the circle upstairs, and because it seats 246 people and Keswick is only a small place, you never have to book in advance.

The Alhambra is a magical relic from another age . . . and an ideal place for a Bongonaut to while away a couple of hours on a wet and windy night.

When I emerged from the Dog and Gun for my short walk to the Alhambra it was a quiet evening, just spotting with rain.

When I came out of the cinema a couple of hours later the rain was hammering on the pavements and a gale was blowing up the street, forcing me to retreat into the foyer while I battled with the zip on my not-very-waterproof fleece.

I walked (I would have run, but my newly-healed broken leg was having none of it) as fast as I could back to the Bongo, and sat in the driver's seat steaming.

I drove through the puddles of the town, back up the hill, found a level parking place just opposite the stone circle and was asleep within half an hour. At two o'clock I woke up, disturbed by the rocking of the van in the wind and the percussion of the rain on the roof.

After so many Bongo Nights I had experience of bad weather, but this was by far the worst I had encountered so far – worse even than the stormy night I had spent looking down from my viewpoint above the Clyde in December.

It was also, in its way, one of the quietest; I didn't see or hear another car from the moment I parked until, at 8.30 am (after only a fitful few hours' sleep) I decided that, no matter what the weather, I simply had to go for a walk around the stone circle.

The sight that met me was extraordinary. Here we were on top of a hill – the last place you would expect to flood – and yet the stone circle was standing in a huge puddle. A lake on top of a hill! I might have wanted to walk around the stones, but it was in fact impossible. The overnight rain, which had clearly been even heavier than I thought, had turned the place into a pond. Castlerigg was no longer a stone circle; it was a Neolithic swimming pool.

I splashed back to the Bongo, took off my dripping cagoule and – with the windscreen wipers on fast – drove home.

36
LAZONBY
Cumbria
Thursday March 5

In the eight days after my visit to Castlerigg I travelled to Somerset (300 miles south) and Aberdeenshire (250 miles north) and slept in six different beds. Little wonder that I didn't have much enthusiasm for going anywhere at all for Bongo Night 36.

But by now my Bongo Nights had achieved their own momentum. So many people knew of the target I had set myself – and so many were even looking forward to find out where my next week's trip would take me – I simply had to go on.

On this night, even though there was nothing I wanted to do less than climb into the Bongo so soon after doing so many miles on the road, duty called. The only allowance I made was that I chose a spot just 15 miles down the road, in the Eden Valley, a part of Cumbria which is still gloriously unspoiled by tourists and tourism.

Between the villages of Lazonby and Kirkoswald, where the road crosses the River Eden on a stately four-arched sandstone bridge, there is a secluded lay-by, presumably used mostly by fishermen and anyone wanting to avail themselves of the recycling skips which – somewhat incongruously for such a remote place, I've always thought

– have been placed there by the local council.

It was not the most scenic, most comfortable or most peaceful place to spend the night, but I was knackered from too much travelling and it was good enough to get the job done.

I made up the bed before I left home, parked the van beside the recycling compound, paused for long enough to enjoy the sound of the river gurgling nearby, and curled up and went to sleep. I might not have slept so well had I known that this was the spot where, just a few weeks before, one of the most poignant of local murder cases had reached its heartbreaking conclusion.

An 82-year-old man had been charged with murdering his 80-year-old wife after she was found dead at their home in a nearby village.

It later emerged that he had asphyxiated her, and tried to kill himself, after the bosses of a local care home – who were supposed to be looking after her while he went into hospital for a minor operation – dumped her back on his doorstep at nine o'clock one evening after deciding her dementia was more than they could cope with.

After spending several weeks in prison on remand awaiting his trial, the old man had been allowed bail. But a few days after being set free he went missing and later, after a huge search, his body was found in the River Eden, very near the spot where I spent the night.

If I had known I would have found some less macabre place in which to sleep – there are, after all, plenty of other very attractive options within a few miles of my home.

As it was, I didn't sleep very well at all. Quite why so many people had to use that road through the night, quite why they needed to do it so noisily, and quite why even more needed to drive into Penrith in a steady stream from about 6.30 in the morning remains something of a mystery.

At least it meant I was awake at seven o'clock when, making even more noise, a council truck arrived to take away the loaded recycling skips and replace them with empty ones.

The driver seemed unconcerned by the fact that I had obviously spent the night there, but even he, I guessed, could not have failed to see a white Bongo beside the aluminium and tin can recycling cage –

or smell the enticing smell of bacon as I gave up hope of any further sleep and started cooking breakfast instead.

He eventually drove away, having failed to speak, wave, answer my "Good Morning" nod or give any other acknowledgement of my presence. Indeed if he had not so studiously avoided eye contact with me I would have thought that he had noticed me at all.

"Miserable sod," I muttered as he disappeared down the road.

37
CRUMMOCK WATER
Cumbria
Friday March 13

Not for the first time, the weather forecast fell a little way short of encouraging. The lucky parts of the country would see rain, and a lot of it; and the unlucky ones would see rain and gales, with perhaps the odd squall of sleet or snow thrown in. It was not a week for a man in his Bongo.

So I set out for the Lake District. The local forecasters suggested that, while most of Cumbria would be suffering under a prolonged period of low pressure, there was just a chance that some sunshine might occasionally break through in the west.

But that good news came with a warning: Too far towards the coast and you'd be pummelled by the gales swinging in from the sea; too far away from it and you'd be in the thick of the cloud and rain. The answer seemed to lie somewhere in the middle, somewhere around Cockermouth – an area I had largely overlooked so far in my Bongo Night challenge. My plan was to head in that direction, stopping off in Cockermouth for some sort of takeaway which I would eat at

Crummock Water before hunkering down for the night in one of the parking places beside the lake and waking next morning perhaps to find I had been blessed with one of the sunny spells the weather man had promised.

The queue in Lee's Chinese takeaway was so long that by the time I had driven the 12 miles to Crummock Water it was so dark that I drove straight past my intended parking spot and ended up instead in the National Trust car park at Buttermere where, back in July, I had had my breakfast after my night on the top of Newlands on Bongo Night 3.

I ate my supper there (a very tasty lemon chicken, fried rice and spring roll) before going back to Crummock Water and – driving more slowly this time – finding a perfect place, well off the road, beside a waterfall and overlooking the lake.

It was only then that I realised the water, which had previously been invisible in the darkness of the valley, was now glistening silver against the dark silhouette of the surrounding fells. The reason I had been able to find my parking place after missing it the first time was that it was now being gently illuminated by the moon shining brightly from a sky full of stars. The promised break in the bad weather had arrived early.

I could only hope that it would last long enough for me to appreciate the view in the morning. It did. I woke early, just as the sun was rising over the mountains behind me, and saw that I had parked in a place which, even in March, would probably soon be busy with walkers arriving in their cars for a day in the hills.

I jumped out of bed, determined to make the most of having it to myself, and went for a short walk, taking great care not to slip and break my leg again as I moved across the wet grass.

It was a perfect morning, with the sun turning the lake a deep blue and picking out the last remnants of snow on the highest parts of the mountains. It was, once again, the sort of morning that made Bongo Nights worthwhile.

But as I returned to the Bongo the first car arrived to spoil it.

It was a dark blue Golf containing just one sour-faced old lady, and she glared at me as her nostrils caught the smell of my cooking bacon, though I was not sure whether it was in disapproval of anyone who dared to spend a night there in a campervan or (more likely I thought) of the world in general. I returned the favour by glaring at her but she played the trump card in our game of early morning ill-feeling by allowing her nasty little white terrier to come over, cock its leg up and pee against the Bongo's front nearside wheel.

38
KIRKCUDBRIGHT
Scotland
Monday March 16

After so many Bongo Nights in such splendid natural scenery I felt like something different, something plainer – rather as I once wanted nothing more than beans on toast after returning from the gastronomic luxury of a Mediterranean cruise.

That's not intended as an insult to Kirkcudbright, which is a delightful, picturesque little place and not "plain" at all, but there's no doubt it is very different from all the wonderful lakes, mountains, beaches and rivers which had formed the backdrop to most of my other trips.

Kirkcudbright is a little gem of a town on the South Scottish coast which is ideal for a night's Bongoing – and not just because they allow campervans to park overnight in the harbour car park there.

It's a joy to walk around – a maze of little streets, some of them cobbled and lined with ancient colourful cottages, with some interesting shops, a National Trust house and garden, several pubs, a first rate chippy and, best of all for someone like me who loves boats, a still active fishing quay.

I had plenty of time so I made a few stops on the way: Dumfries (a town which I suspected must be much more pleasant than for some reason I had always found it to be), New Abbey (which has an excellent antique shop in which I had hoped to find a kitchen chair to suit our new kitchen at home) and Rockcliffe (a little seaside village, from which several lovely walks radiate out from its tiny car park).

In Dumfries I had a walk along the river, and explored enough to establish that it is indeed a more attractive place than I had ever given it credit for.

In New Abbey I found all kinds of antique treasures (including a 17th century carved oak chair which I could and would have bought for £240 if only we had had somewhere in our house to put it).

And in Rockcliffe I went for a walk.

I knew the path that led to Kippford, the next village – something of a tourist hot spot, which has a lovely pub overlooking the river – but reckoned that was probably too far for a just-recovered broken leg, so I took another one into the woods which I hoped would be a little less strenuous.

I was studying details of several signposted walks on a map embedded in a rock, and trying to decide which one to take, when I was joined by a couple of my age (my guess, from what they were saying, was that she lived locally and he was her new boyfriend, to whom she was showing the local sights).

I asked their advice, explaining that I was not very confident on my feet.

"This is my first proper walk for two months so I don't want anything too difficult," I said. "I've broken one leg and I don't want to break the other."

The woman pointed to a circular walk on the map which she reckoned would suit me.

"It's a good firm surface, and there are no steep hills, so you should be all right," she said.

I thanked her, and told her that after such good local advice I would give it a go.

"Don't blame us if it all goes terribly wrong," her partner laughed. "If you break your leg and try to sue us we'll say we don't live around here, we don't know you and we've never ever met you before in our lives."

He walked off briskly, still chuckling at his joke, as I followed, limping slightly, more slowly behind.

The path wound through the woods and up – via the sort of climb I would not have dared tackle only a week before – to a viewpoint.

I felt on top of the world in more ways than one. Sure enough, it was a magnificent view over the estuary. But better than that, I had managed to walk there, and walking was still something that filled my heart with joy.

The path would have gone on, steeply down between rocks on the other side until it reached the Kippford path nearer the sea, and it was one I would have followed without a thought a few months before.

But this time I was more hesitant. I was not confident enough on my feet for such a scramble, so I turned round, headed back the way I had come and found an easier route.

When I arrived at the Bongo I had been walking for nearly 90 minutes and was pleased to see that, according to the map, I had covered around three miles. I had got my freedom back!

Kirkcudbright was just as delightful as I remembered, though since my last visit they had erected barriers on the harbourside so it was no longer possible for campervans (or anyone else apart from accredited fishermen) to park right beside the boats. Even so, the main car park was perfectly acceptable, being just a stone's throw from the river.

I chose a parking place taking into account as many criteria as I could – near the boats, fairly close (but not too close) to the public toilets, on a level site and in a position in which the inevitable street lights were not going to shine too brightly through the Bongo's curtains – locked up and went for a walk.

This quickly established that the award winning Polarbites fish and chip shop – one of the reasons I had chosen to go to Kirkcudbright – was closed because it was Monday.

The only alternative (apart from cooking my own supper, which of course I could easily have done had I had the inclination) was to eat in one of the several pubs dotted along the town's pretty streets.

And that only served to highlight one of the problems of spending Bongo Nights in Scotland – the new drink-driving laws, which have reduced the amount of alcohol a driver is allowed to have consumed.

The new laws, which came into effect on December 24 2014, mean that, whereas a driver can get away with drinking more than a pint of beer in England, the same amount will put him substantially over the limit in Scotland.

And since my understanding of the law is that "driver" means anyone who is in charge of a vehicle – whether or not he has any intention of actually driving it – it would include a man spending the night in his campervan in a Kirkcudbright car park.

Now, I know the chance of a policeman coming knocking on my Bongo to give me a breath test in the middle of the night is pretty remote, but it is a chance I am not prepared to take.

I could envisage some bored constable, who is falling behind with his quota of arrests, deciding to blitz the car park in the almost certain knowledge that he would find some sleeping miscreant in a campervan there.

"A pint of orange juice and lemonade, please," I told the young barman at the Kirkcudbright Bay Hotel, an establishment I had chosen purely on the basis that, after walking twice around the town, it was the last pub I came to before I arrived back at the harbour .

I explained that, though I wasn't planning on driving, I wasn't taking any chances.

"We get a lot of people like that," he told me. "We sell a lot of soft drinks these days."

After an excellent meal – chicken stuffed with haggis (well, I was in Scotland!) – I left the pub completely sober and went for another walk around the town.

In fact, during my few hours in Kirkcudbright I walked round the place five times – twice as soon as I got there, once in the evening twilight after leaving the pub, once in the dark and once when the sun came up next morning. Not bad for someone who, just a few weeks earlier, had not been able to walk at all!

39
SEATHWAITE
Cumbria
Friday March 27

In my 39th week there was only one night when I was not too busy to go off in the Bongo – and the weather forecast for that night was simply appalling. Although the afternoon and early evening promised to be calm and sunny, we were being warned not to be fooled. A tremendous amount of rain was on its way overnight, and it would continue for most of the next morning.

In such circumstances there was only one thing to do: Head for the wettest place in England.

Seathwaite is a tiny hamlet (little more than a single farm actually) which is renowned as having more rain in a typical year than any other inhabited place in the country.

London gets around 25 inches of rain a year, and most of the rest of the country doesn't get much more. Seathwaite in Borrowdale gets 140 inches.

So with the promise of truly terrible weather I felt the need to confront it head on. It would, after all, be something to boast about: "I was in my Bongo in the wettest place in England on the wettest night of the year."

Imagine my disappointment when I arrived and found the sun was shining.

I knew that along the road leading into Seathwaite (it's a dead end) were several good places for a night's wild camping, and I found one of them on a roomy gravel area near a farm gateway about a quarter of a mile from the village, just before the wide grassy verge on which several cars had been left while their owners were walking on the high fells.

With the sun shining down from a clear blue sky I parked the Bongo, then continued on foot into the valley – along the road to where it ends, past a group of farm buildings and along a track beside a river – determined to make the most of whatever good weather the fates were going to allow me.

My gentle walk took me past the farm, where an inexpertly painted sign pointed into a field: "Parking all day £3, all night £5."

Another sign pointed to showers and toilets, while another admitted "No modern facilities" (leaving me to wonder what facilities the owners of a small campsite in the middle of nowhere felt they should apologise for not having).

So here was a farmer trying to make a few bob by setting a field aside for campers – people such as I. And there was I, planning to deprive him of that very small windfall by parking on a rough piece of land just up the road.

I looked around for the farmer, and eventually spotted him as he drove out of the farmyard with four sheep in a trailer on the back of a quadbike.

I waved him down.

"I was planning to spend the night in my campervan just up there," I told him, gesturing up the lane to where the white roof of the Bongo could just be seen above the hedge. "But that would just be bloody mean, wouldn't it – parking up there just so I didn't have to pay you your fiver?"

He pushed back his woolly hat and gave his head a scratch. "You're a gentleman," he said. "Thank you. There should be more people like you."

He told me to park wherever I liked in the field, but warned me I might not necessarily have it all to myself for the whole night.

"There was someone else here," he said. "Last Tuesday, I think."

I told him I thought nobody else would be daft enough to want to spend the night in Seathwaite with such bad weather forecast.

"I might need you to come with your tractor to pull me out if I get stuck in the mud in the morning," I said.

He assured me he would be happy to help, but doubted that he would need to.

"The field's all right," he said.

The rain started at about 2am, just gentle at first, though enough to wake me as it drummed on the Bongo's roof. By 6am it was pounding so hard I could not hear the radio that I had turned on when I realised I stood no chance of getting back to sleep.

By 8am, as I cooked my breakfast, I noticed that puddles were beginning to form in the "all right" field.

I had gone to Seathwaite hoping for some dramatic wet weather . . . and I had got it. It was all rather exciting, but a little worrying at the same time. Much as I liked this little village, and much as I had warmed to the farmer who lived there, I had no wish to be stuck there, trapped on the wrong side of a waterlogged field.

I ate my bacon and egg faster than was probably good for me, packed everything away in an untidy jumble in the back of the van and ran round to the driver's door.

I had only run from one side of the van to the other, but by the time I was sitting behind the steering wheel I was soaked to the skin.

I plotted a course across the field, heading for small patches which my memory told me had been reinforced with rubble and using them as stepping stones between the deeper puddles.

It was with some relief that I reached the other side and felt the wheels gripping the firmness of the farmyard.

"Good morning!" the farmer shouted when he spotted me as he came out of one of his barns.

"I told you it was going to rain," I laughed as I wound down the window.

"Yes, this is quite good even by our standards. Mind out, you'll get wet, better close the window."

I said nothing, but glanced down at my soaking trousers.

"Ah, too late, I see," he said.

And so it was that I had quite a lengthy chat with the farmer – he apparently not noticing that he did not even have a coat on, and I ignoring the fact that it was raining inside the Bongo almost as hard as it was outside it.

"See you again," he called as I wished him goodbye.

"I hope so – but it will never be as exciting as this," I told him.

40
RIBBLEHEAD
Yorkshire Dales
Thursday April 2

High up in the Yorkshire hills, between Kirkby Stephen and Settle on the famous Settle-Carlisle railway line, lies the charming little Ribblehead railway station – a station which exists, it seems to me, purely for the benefit of the thousands of walkers who like to spend their spare time exploring the Yorkshire Dales.

There are precious few houses in the vicinity, but just down the lane, and across the surprisingly busy main road, is the Station Hotel, a huge rambling building which, in high season, is packed with tourists and muddy boots.

It is also, I now know, a pub well known for allowing campervans to park overnight in its ample car park.

I had no idea of all this until a friend, making a journey on the railway from Carlisle to Leeds, happened to look out of the train window at the right time and spotted several vans in the pub car park.

She sent me a message immediately: "Good place for a Bongo Night."

It just happened that at that time I was looking for somewhere in that area in which to spend the night. The football season was coming towards its close, Bristol City were still top of the table and heading inexorably, incredibly towards promotion and the next match was away at Oldham Athletic – a game I could easily combine with a night in the Bongo.

Although I timed my journey so that I would be arriving at Ribblehead in mid afternoon, by the time I got there the pub car park was full. True, half of it was taken up by a huge marquee, but the rest of it was crammed with four enormous mobile homes, with another Bongo squeezed in between them.

A quick glance told me that there would be no room for me – indeed the vans already there were parked so closely together that their occupants would barely be able to open their doors without clouting the vehicle next door.

And – though there were several lay-bys and pull-ins in the vicinity – most of those were full of cars and the odd campervan too.

I drove up the road and back again, and settled eventually on an informal lay-by, which allowed me enough space to pull in well off the road.

It was not what I had anticipated, but it was better than nothing – and it had an excellent view of all 24 arches of the Ribblehead viaduct as it carried the railway line across Batty Moss 100 feet below.

In fact, I discovered that by chance I had parked beside a rough path that led over the moorland directly to the viaduct, with all of the Yorkshire Dales' famous Three Peaks – Pen-y-Ghent, Ingleborough and Whernside – looming in the near distance.

I spent more than an hour there – gazing up at the viaduct while sitting on a grassy hill on the site of the camp where nearly 1,000 navvies once lived while building this incredible bridge nearly 150 years ago – before realising it was time to pay a visit to the pub where, I hoped, I'd be able to get a meal if not somewhere to camp.

The bar was full of families – noisy, excited children who stopped running around the place only when great plates full of sausage, beans and chips were placed in front of them – and I tried to work out which, if any, belonged to the motorhomes outside.

I bought a pint, ordered a steak and kidney pudding, sat on a bar stool and tried – and failed – to start a conversation with either the barman or the leather-skinned old lady who was sipping her stout from a personalised pewter tankard.

As always, my first pint slipped down almost without my noticing it, so I asked for another . . . and when the barman reached for a clean glass told him I was quite happy to drink it out of my dirty one.

That, bizarrely, was all it took for the old lady to decide that perhaps I was someone worth talking to after all.

"Daft isn't it?" she said. "They all do it these days. What do they think – that we might catch our own germs. Daft. I expect it's Europe."

Now I am rather in favour of our relationship with Europe, and reckon that most of the bad publicity aimed at the EU is down to the bias of whichever newspaper is behind it, but I was not in the mood for arguing politics with a half-drunk old lady I'd only just met.

Instead I agreed with her wholeheartedly (with the daftness of it all, if not the political finger-pointing behind it) and kept the conversation going

"Are you local then?" I asked, gesturing at her tankard.

"As local as anyone is, I suppose," she replied.

"She's like a bad smell," the barman joined in. "We try to get rid of her but she just keeps coming back."

"Yeah, that's me," she laughed. "Nothing more than a bad smell."

She asked me what I was doing there – clearly a man on his own at the start of a bank holiday weekend was something to be inquired about – so I told her I had a camper van just up the road, and would be spending the night there since there was obviously no chance of finding a space anywhere better.

"You didn't want to go there anyway – not in the pub car park and not in any of the lay-bys either," she told me.

"Oh, didn't I?"

"No. And you don't want to stay where you are now, either. All too noisy. You'd never sleep."

"Oh?" I thought a raised eyebrow was all that was now required, and I was right.

"There's a much better place. Just nobody knows about it."

I said nothing.

"Go out of here, under the bridge and turn straight left. Up there. That's where I'd go."

So I did. And she was right. I took the Bongo under the bridge and turned left, as instructed, and found myself on a road which ran parallel to the railway line until it ended in a small car park, ostensibly for a nature reserve, immediately opposite the station.

It was, as the old lady had suggested, a perfect place for a campervan – secluded without being isolated, with wonderful views in all directions, and apparently unnoticed even by the rucsac-carrying ramblers who found their way onto the station platform every half hour or so until it got dark.

By the time I left after a leisurely breakfast next morning I had seen precious few people and not a single car. But as I drove away on the road to Settle (and Oldham) I noticed a burger van in one of the lay-bys, with a queue of people already lined up beside it.

I got to Oldham in good time – early enough to take a walk around the uninspiring town centre and still arrive at the Boundary Park football ground a couple of hours before the kick off. I had parked neatly in the car park when a serious-faced woman in a high visibility jacket came knocking on my window to tell me that because the Bongo was "a bus" I would have to move it and park it instead in the official coach park, sandwiched between the huge Bristol City team coach and the fleet of matching supporters' buses alongside it.

I told her I would be delighted to do so, and joked that there could be no greater thrill for a Bongo-owning Bristol City supporter to be given such an honour. She looked puzzled (Oldham Athletic's high visibility car park wardens seem not to have a sense of humour) but not as puzzled as when I asked if, after the match, I would be able to join the coaches as the police on motorbikes escorted them in a convoy away from the ground.

For the record: The match ended in a 1-1 draw, leaving City a hard-to-believe eight points clear at the top of the league. And I did not need a police escort home.

41
MUNGRISDALE
Cumbria
Thursday April 9

Experience has told me that nobody in his right mind goes out on the roads in the week after Easter – especially when the weather is fine and, like me, he lives on the fringes of the Lake District.

But on this occasion I didn't have much choice: My younger son was moving home – from one Lake District village to another – and needed my Bongo to transport some of his furniture which had been being stored temporarily at my house And anyway, experience has also told me that even in Cumbria there are some places within easy reach of my home which are, as yet, undiscovered by the tourists.

And so it was that for my 41st Bongo Night I headed for Mungrisdale, a tiny village which gives its name to a wild open valley on the northern fringes of the Lake District. It is a place that the thousands of drivers never see as they scurry along the A66 road towards their honeypot destinations further into the mountains. But – apart from the fact that there are no lakes to delight the eyes of the photographers among them – it is just as beautiful as any of its better known cousins.

And, as I was delighted to confirm when I found my parking place among the gorse bushes, it's a damn sight quieter.

The spot I chose was an area about the size of a tennis court, perfectly flat and enclosed by gorse, with nothing but a small farm in the dim distance. Years before Tricia and I had had a picnic there, and I had resolved to return sometime to spend the night. Now I was back. And it was every bit as beautiful as I had remembered.

The sun was still high in the sky and there was nothing more than a gentle breeze floating across the valley – perfect conditions, I reckoned, for my first bike ride since breaking my leg.

I enjoy cycling (though only over pitifully small distances when compared with some of my more exuberantly fit friends) but I was still cautious of what I asked my leg to do, so I had not been on my bike for several months.

However, the idea of Bongoing in the Mungrisdale valley had persuaded me this would be a good time to load my bike onto the back of the Bongo, just in case . . .

The valley is ideal for cycling – flat enough to be not too much of a challenge, but hilly enough at least to make me puff a bit.

I cycled just a couple of miles down the road, then turned round and cycled back again.

When I returned to the Bongo my leg, which still tended to swell and hurt a bit by the day's end, was feeling better than it had at any time since I'd broken it.

My evening – marvelling at the view, playing my guitar, cooking pasta and meatballs and listening to the radio – saw me in happy mood, and when I awoke at six o'clock next morning I couldn't wait to get out on my bike again. This time I rode just a little further, but again caution made me turn back before my leg got tired.

But, with no damage done, after breakfast I did the same ride again – it was such a lovely road there was no point finding any other route, and anyway the changing light made it seem different every time.

On my way back to the Bongo I was overtaken by a car – the first sign of life I had seen since parking the evening before.

Just a few miles from the tourist chaos of the Lake District I had indeed found a truly beautiful undiscovered place.

I allowed myself to feel just a little bit smug.

42
PAXTON HOUSE
Near Berwick upon Tweed
Wednesday April 15

One of the reasons that Tricia accompanied me on only a few Bongo Nights was that we realise that it's good – especially now we are both retired – for a couple not to spend every hour of every day together. Another one is that, while I am happy to hide behind a bush to answer nature's call, she prefers to have something at least approaching basic toilet facilities.

So when I had a hankering to go to the North-East coast (an area she is particularly fond of) I resolved to find a "proper" campsite, so that she would be comfortable coming with me.

I soon found just such a place – a small caravan site with a touch of quirkiness thanks to its location inside the walled garden of a stately home.

Paxton House is an 18th century John Adam mansion standing in its own 80 acres of woodland and grounds on the northern bank of the River Tweed (and therefore in Scotland), a few miles inland from Berwick-upon-Tweed (which is in England).

Its caravan park is a Caravan Club CL (Certificated Location), so it is allowed to accommodate no more than five campervans or caravans even though the walled garden in which it is set is big enough to hold several dozen.

It sounded ideal so I booked a pitch immediately.

It took me a day to remember that not all CLs have toilets (I had been caught out by this before but had forgotten) and, on closer examination, Paxton House was one that did not.

By then we were all geared up to go, so we had to make a few quick decisions: Should we cancel the booking (even at the risk of losing the money I had already paid for it), should I try to amend it, so that we would both go somewhere else that night, with me returning to the toilet-less Paxton House alone on some other occasion, or should we continue as planned and simply put up with the lack of facilities?

We decided on the latter, largely on the basis that with 80 acres of grounds and woodland there would surely be a tree or a bush somewhere behind which Tricia could hide behind in complete privacy. And are we glad we did!

Paxton House and its grounds were glorious. There could surely have been hardly a better place to go on a summer's day . . . or night.After a hearty lunch in the visitors' teashop we spent a couple of hours walking around the estate, watching the birds from a hide beside the river and just sitting enjoying all the best that a British garden can offer on a perfect summer's day. We cycled into the nearby village (primarily, it has to be said, to find out where the pub was, so that we'd know where to go for our supper), took another stroll around the garden and popped into the teashop once again for afternoon tea (and to use the customers' toilets before they closed).In the evening we cycled to the pub, and found it to be closed, so returned to the Bongo for a hasty meal of meatballs and pasta before taking another walk around the grounds.Sleeping in a mansion's walled garden was just as delightfully eccentric as we'd hoped and without doubt will be as close as I'm ever going to get to living in a stately home.

That would have been enough. If we had woken to heavy rain next morning, and gone straight home after breakfast we would have been satisfied. But there was much more.

We woke to bright sunshine, so even before breakfast we were walking yet again around the grounds. The gardens, the woodland and the river were all looking magnificent in the early morning light – especially the river, which sparkled in the sun as we walked along the bank.

"Stop!" whispered Tricia.

She has remarkable eyesight on such occasions, and while I could have walked up and down the river without noticing anything, she had spotted a ripple, some unexplained activity on the far river bank. "Otters!"

Neither of us had ever seen river otters before, though we had seen them – briefly – playing on the rocks on one of our Scottish seaside holidays, but this was very different.

There were three of them – a mother and two babies probably – playing on the mud and between the reeds on the bank opposite, and we watched them for more than an hour, slowly walking down the path on our side of the river as they made their way downstream on theirs.

We returned to the Bongo in a state of some excitement knowing that one of the advantages of sleeping in a small campervan – which even I will admit does not afford the best night's sleep for two people – was that we had woken so early that we were out walking at the only time of the day to see an animal that neither of us had properly seen before.

And that, if nothing else, had made our trip to Paxton House worthwhile. With or without a flush lavatory.

43
HAY-ON-WYE
Powys, Wales
Tuesday April 21

Hay-on-Wye is a magical little town famous these days for a book festival which brings far too many tourists (though they'd no doubt like to call themselves literary intellectuals) to its narrow streets every year.

It is also the gateway for some spectacular scenery – the Black Mountains to the west, and, if you can find the turning that leads you to it, a spectacularly wild road over open moorland which eventually winds down to the village of Llanthony and its ancient priory to the south.

It was there to which I was heading for my 43rd Bongo Night as I wound my way on a scenic route through mid Wales to see my mother in Somerset.

Even though the evening sun was shining when I got there, Hay looked rather sad, I thought, as if it somehow expected something rather more from the few tourists who seemed to be doing nothing more than waiting for the time when it would be appropriate to go back for an early night at their B&Bs.

Certainly none of them seemed to be keen to spend any money, and when, after a quick walk around the town, I ventured into the Three Tuns pub I had the place to myself.

"You're very quiet," I said to the barmaid, aware that I was stating the blooming obvious.

"Yeah," she said without looking up from the game she was playing on her mobile, and I wondered if everyone else who wanted a pint had gone up the road to some other establishment where the staff were rather more welcoming.

"Maybe it's a bit early," I ventured.

"Yeah."

She assured me – by saying "Yeah" to each of my following questions – that it would be possible to have some food to go with my pint of some unheard-of Welsh ale, so I ordered a "slow-cooked piece of tasty brisket", which was presented to me with little ceremony in little more than the time it takes to say "microwave oven". It was, it's fair to say, a very tasty "slow-cooked piece of tasty brisket", served on a dollop of well mashed potato surrounded by red cabbage, but neither it nor the barmaid detained me for very long.

Using the satnav on my mobile phone I was able to follow a convoluted route to the road that eventually, after threatening to disappear into a couple of farms, emerged triumphantly out the other side and led me to the mountain road I was aiming for.

Sure enough, it was exactly as I had hoped: a narrow road which cut across the top of the moor, with wonderful views of the sun setting over the valley and the far hills of the Brecon Beacons.

I drove for several miles, making a mental note of potential places to spend the night (but ignoring a large, well-kept tarmac lay-by on the grounds that it looked too much like a place where the local dogging enthusiasts might meet in their cars later on) then turned around when the road started winding downhill towards Llanthony.

I eventually disregarded a few gravel-strewn parking places, and settled instead for a flattish piece of grass among the gorse, where I could park facing the setting sun.

I spent a long time leaning against the front of the Bongo, watching the sun going down, smiled and waved at the few people passing in their cars and was pleased to see that a farmer waved in equally friendly fashion when he passed on his quadbike – a good sign that nobody would object to my spending the night there, I thought.

Soon I was joined by half a dozen sheep and a couple of ponies, and I fetched my guitar from the back and serenaded them until it got so cold I had to close the door.

44
HARDKNOTT
Cumbria
Thursday April 30

There are many times when I am glad to own a Bongo rather than any other campervan or (mutter the words quietly) motorhome.

Finding myself half-way up the Hardknott Pass in the Lake District was one of them.

Hardknott is renowned as the most difficult of all the Cumbrian passes.

It is very narrow, boasts a series of hairpin bends and is extraordinarily steep in some places, reaching a height of 393m (1,289ft) before it plunges in a series of even sharper bends down towards the Wrynose Pass on the other side. Indeed it is so steep that its 1 in 3 gradient earns it the title – shared with Rosedale Chimney Bank in North Yorkshire – of the steepest road in England.

It is on the far side of the Lake District from where I live, a good two hours' drive away, so it's a place I have not bothered to go to very often.

On this occasion though I had plenty of time, the weather forecast was good and – most important – I felt it was time for a little exploration.

It was unfortunate that such exploration took me towards the threatening monstrosity that's the Sellafield nuclear reprocessing site . . . and, in particular, the many hundreds of people who at that precise moment were knocking off after a day working there and who, it seems, believe they own the road along which I was driving.

My route took me along the narrow country road which skirts the mountains between Ennerdale Bridge and the coast and which just happens to be the rat run used, it seems, by most of the Sellafield workforce on their way home.

I met the first of them just after Ennerdale Bridge, and over the next five miles there were (and I'm not exaggerating) more than a hundred others.

Every one of them was driving too fast. Every one of them – mostly middle-aged men in ties and well-pressed shirts – passed me without acknowledgement or any sign that they were even aware that I had pulled onto the verge to get out of out of their way. And every one of them got my back up.

The sensible thing, I suppose, would have been for me to pull into a lay-by, make a cup of tea and calmly admire the view while this selfish convoy of arrogance made its way home.

But instead, after the first few dozen had passed, I had had enough.

No more pulling into a passing place as soon as I spotted them coming in the distance. From then on I was going to remind them that I had as much right to be on that road as they did.

My leisurely drive along that lovely road became a pointless – and, I admit, childish – game of chicken, seeing who had the courage (or bloody-mindedness, anyway) to give way last. It's true that I almost always lost, but at least I had the satisfaction of making them slow down.

And it was only towards the end, after I had pulled into a farm gateway to make way for a little blue Toyota, that a driver lifted a hand and smiled "Thank you" as she passed.

She was a young woman, with cropped blonde hair and a huge stud in her nose, and I was so surprised by her good manners that I wanted to get out and kiss her.

Soon afterwards I called in for a walk on the beach at the little Victorian resort of Seascale (just down the road from Sellafield) before turning inland into Eskdale and on towards Hardknott, where I planned to spend the night.

The roadsigns warned me that the road was not for the faint-hearted, with advice that it should only be attempted by drivers in "light vehicles".

I have always boasted that the Bongo can go anywhere a car can go, so I ignored them, with a familiar smug feeling growing inside me since I knew that anything bigger (the sort of motorhomes that tow small cars in their wake, for example) would have had to turn back.

As I ventured further up the hill the scenery became spectacularly beautiful – wilder and more rugged than the Lake District valleys I was so used to closer to home – and I was so mesmerised by the view unfolding in front of me that I missed the lay-by I was aiming for.

I had decided to park at the Hardknott Roman fort – a cluster of ruins which is all that's left of the military buildings which guarded the Romans' "Tenth Highway" in the 2nd century – but in my excitement I was at the top of the hill before I realised I had driven straight past it.

The top of Hardknott pass is no place to attempt a three-point turn, so I had no option but to continue all the way down the other side, where I was at last able to turn at the junction where the road widened out to accommodate a bigger one coming up the valley from the right.

I went back the way I had come, but somehow the road seemed steeper, and the bends sharper than they had on the way down, and even the Bongo seemed to be having second thoughts about making it.

It seemed to be telling me that once over Hardknott had been quite fun, but going back for a second go to do it all again was beyond the call of duty.

We made it though, and not for the first time I was glad to be in a Bongo rather than anything bigger or less dependable.

I eventually found the car park I was looking for – much further from the top of the hill than I expected – and I reversed into it, adjusting my position just a little bit to find the most level area.

I got out and for the first time got a good look at the place in which I had chosen to spend the night.

Behind me (in the direction from which I had just come) was the road snaking haphazardly up Hardknott, to my left was the imposing great mass of Harter Fell, and to my right the majestic peaks – still covered in snow – of Scafell Pike, England's highest mountain.

But it was the view ahead of me – ten miles back down the valley towards the coast, where just a couple of hours before I had been walking on the beach – which, quite literally, took my breath away and brought tears to my eyes.

I was inside a horse-shoe of grand mountains, with the open end directing my gaze over ten miles of magnificent scenery and on into the distant sea, which dazzled brightly in the sunshine like a diamond bracelet around the Isle of Man.

This, I decided, was the most dramatic location for a Bongo Night since I had stood on Malin Head seven months before.

And the weather was perfect. The evening sunshine was golden and warm, bathing the view in ever-changing colours until it disappeared behind the fell in a spectacular cascade of reds, oranges and purples.

I spent a little time exploring the fort (much bigger than I had expected) but mostly I spent the evening sitting on a grass-capped rocky ridge a few yards from the Bongo.

I read a book there, had my supper there and played my guitar there, all the while gazing at the extraordinary view in front of me.

Only a few cars passed, creeping past in bottom gear as they negotiated a particularly steep hairpin bend, and – just as the sun turned into its most golden and I sat clutching my guitar on my knees – one of them stopped. The driver, a middle-aged man with his hands clasped at the top of his steering wheel as if he was saying a prayer, put his head out of his window.

"That's the most beautiful place any man could ever hope to play his guitar," he said.

"That's what I've been thinking for at least two hours now," I told him with a grin.

45
SAMYE LING BUDDHIST TEMPLE
Scottish Borders
Tuesday May 5

With most of my Bongo nights I have little idea where I am going until a few minutes before I leave home.

A quick look at the map, a glance at the weather forecast and I'll be off, heading to where the sunshine is expected to be the brightest (or the rain the least).

But sometimes a little planning is required – if only to make sure I don't arrive in my chosen location to find that it's already full, closed down or been turned into a supermarket.

The trouble with planning a Bongo Night long in advance, though, is that you never have any idea what the weather's going to be like when the day arrives.

Which is how Tricia and I came to be visiting the Samye Ling Tibetan Buddhist centre on what was almost certainly the wettest day of what had been a very wet year.

It was pouring with rain when we arrived at this wonderful place hidden away in the beautiful countryside of the Scottish Borders near Eskdalemuir, a few miles from Langholm. It was pouring with rain when we left the next day . . . and it had been pouring with rain virtually every minute in between.

I would be lying if I said the weather did not come close to ruining the visit.

Ever since our visit to the Kadampa Buddhist temple at Conishead Priory after my very first Bongo Night, I had nursed the ambition to spend some time at Samye Ling, which is both better known and in an even more beautiful part of the country.

I knew that even if they had no interest in Buddhism visitors were welcome to stay overnight in the very basic tent campsite there, and a brief exchange of emails confirmed that campervans would be received equally happily, if they parked in the car park, though it was recommended that an advance booking should be made just in case.

"Many people join us for a quiet, relaxing break, to experience life in the monastery for a while or to use it as a base for exploring the local countryside," the monk in charge of the reception desk wrote. "Guests don't have to be attending a course in order to stay, nor do they have to attend group prayer or meditation sessions, although they are welcome to do so if they wish."

That sounded precisely the sort of basis upon which I wanted to visit.

And I was very happy to agree to the list of conditions – including refraining from killing, lying and any form of sexual misconduct – that accompanied the confirmation that I had been allocated an overnight space in the monastery car park.

We were already dripping by the time we arrived to check in and hand over the £36 that would cover not just the parking but also supper, breakfast and lunch in the monastery canteen (did I mention that it was raining?).

So we were relieved to hear that, because very few visitors were expected that day, we would be allowed to park inside the monastery rather than in the car park which was a good five minutes' soggy walk away.

The shaven-headed monk behind the desk told us we were free to wander where we liked, and were welcome to attend any prayer or meditation sessions if we wished.

Even so, it's difficult to know what to do in a monastery when you

arrive in a downpour at two o'clock in the afternoon.
 I had imagined a gentle afternoon, strolling around the grounds in the sunshine, relaxing on benches in the gardens, watching the world go by and . . . well, meditating.
 But all those things are difficult to do when the rain's dribbling your neck, so we headed to the Tibetan Tea Room to collect our thoughts over a hot chocolate instead.
 "We're British, dammit, we're not going to let a bit of rain spoil our day," we said as we emerged out into the gardens.
 And so we spent the afternoon – cagoules tightly zipped, hoods up – exploring the place. We spent some time in the temple, we explored the covered walkway where you can pay to have your remains (and those of your pets) kept for eternity, and we even hop-scotched around the puddles to explore the peace and herb gardens.
 We wanted to experience Buddhist prayers during our visit so after a simple supper – soup and delicious home-made bread – we followed a few other people for chenrezig evening prayers, which unusually that day were being held not in the main temple but in a beautiful pagoda-shaped stupa nearby.
 We soon found out why.
 For inside the shrine, standing on a pair of wooden trestles, was a small coffin.
 Just a few days previously one of the monastery nuns had died, and here she was lying in readiness for her funeral the next day.
 Undeterred, we sat along the four walls of the stupa, with the coffin in the middle – two nuns and a monk on one side, with the rest of us (a handful of Buddhist followers who clearly knew both the ropes sitting cross-legged on the floor and Tricia and I, who didn't, perching on chairs) on the three other sides
 It is not usual to spend an hour sitting around the coffin of someone you don't know, in the company of people you've never met before, who are tunelessly chanting words which sound as if they are taken

from the menu of your local Indian takeaway.

On one level it was uncomfortably surreal if not slightly macabre. But on another level it was perfectly magical. Within a few minutes it seemed the most lovely, natural thing in the world.

And not for the first time in such surroundings, I found myself transported to an almost mindless state of relaxation.

But still the rain fell. And we awoke next morning to even deeper puddles, even more mud and even less likelihood of being able to enjoy the tranquillity of the garden.

After breakfast (porridge and toast) and a drenching walk beside the river we decided to cut our losses.

We had enjoyed our visit to Samye Ling and had relished some extraordinary experiences, but – although it meant missing the lunch that we'd already paid for – we'd had enough.

As we drove away from Eskdalemuir it was still raining. Hard.

46
ISLE OF WHITHORN
Scotland
Wednesday May 20

Another week in which family business meant I had to travel to Somerset before going home for one night, only to head further north to Aberdeenshire, left no time for a Bongo Night – which meant I had to do two nights the following week just to catch up.

A two-night break gave me the opportunity to venture slightly further afield than usual . . . so I found myself heading along the south Scotland coast, past Carsethorn (Bongo Night No 2), Drumburn (No 32) and Kirkcudbright (No 38) and towards somewhere even more special.

This is an area which is just as beautiful as Cornwall or the West Coast of Scotland, but much less known than either. To say it is unspoiled is to do a disservice to that word.

Great sandy beaches, rocky coves, pretty fishing villages . . . it is my sort of place.

But even there, amid such beauty, there is tragedy.

For the third time in my Bongo Night adventure I found myself parked among memories of tragedy and death.

Unlike Marsden Moor and my spot beside the River Eden, this one was not blighted by murder, but by maritime disaster.

Isle of Whithorn – not an island at all, but a village – is the place from which seven local men sailed on a scallop dredger called the Solway Harvester on a tragic voyage in January 2000 which ended amid lasting suspicion and recrimination.

The crew – two of them just 17 years old – died together when the boat capsized and sank in a Force 9 gale off the coast of Ramsey on the Isle of Man.

An official inquiry later found that the boat had filled with water – at least partly because of "critical maintenance issues" which meant a hatch cover was missing and a flood alarm was not working.

The boat's owner Richard Gidney was put on trial for manslaughter but cleared when the case against him collapsed in 2005.

But in November 2008 a coroner, while ruling the deaths of all seven crew members were accidental, was severely critical of him over the boat's standard of maintenance and equipment, as well as her past safety record.

Even though I knew a little of Isle of Whithorn's sad history, the sight of the two tasteful memorials – a marble bench erected by the Freemasons, and a rather more evocative stone beside an anchor on the headland overlooking the harbour – brought me up short.

That such tragedy could befall such a tranquil, beautiful place just seemed to make that tragedy worse.

Isle of Whithorn is a small village built in a horseshoe around the harbour, with the far end leading past a pub, around a corner to a small car park from which a footpath winds through a well equipped children's playground towards a grassy headland upon which sits a bizarre white-painted square construction which has been used for hundreds of years as a signalling tower.

It was in that car park, with the Bongo facing out towards the inrushing tide, that I chose to spend the night.

It was, perhaps, not quite as idyllic as it sounds – I was parked beside a dog shit bin, close to a dilapidated caravan and in the shadow of some buildings which were in such a state of dereliction it was impossible to tell whether they had once been houses, shops or warehouses.

In normal circumstances the ageing Portacabin housing the single public lavatory would also have to be added to that list of decay, but in this case it would be unfair, for this toilet – unusually for such a primitive structure – was beautifully maintained and clean, with a full complement of toilet paper, running water, paper towels . . . and a locking door. And what's more it was open all night.

The first thing that has to be done in such a village is to explore, so I spent a good hour wandering around and strolling out to the headland, which I could not help but notice was covered in a remarkable carpet of wild flowers.

They tossed their heads lazily in the evening sunshine, the sea was deep blue and calm and a hare was so confident in its safety that it didn't even bother to run away as I passed.

Such a lovely place deserves a lovely pub . . . and in the Steam Packet Inn it has one.

I was able to sit at a table in the window, with the last rays of the day's sun streaming onto me like the spotlight on the leading actor in a West End play, and ordered a pint of orange juice and lemonade (I was still wary of drinking any alcohol, for the same reasons that had condemned me to a temporary state of teetotalness in Kirkcudbright on Bongo Night No 38) and waited for my "smoked haddock and black pudding wrapped in bacon and served on a bed of mushroom risotto with a cullen skink sauce".

And delicious it all was!

I slept well that night, undisturbed by anything at all until I was woken at 5am by the sound of a trawler – appropriately called the Bright Horizon – thrugging out on the morning tide.

I pulled back the curtain and saw that, though the sun was not yet shining, it was obvious it soon would be, so I got up . . . and headed back to the headland, where I sat for an hour on a bench, hoping that an odd whale or basking shark might choose that moment to pass by below me. It didn't. Which proves only that even in a place as magical as Isle of Whithorn you can't have everything.

47
MULL OF GALLOWAY
Scotland
Thursday May 21

As I arrived at Scotland's most southerly point my mobile phone flashed me a text message welcoming me to the Isle of Man and warning me of the expensive consequences if I chose to go "roaming" on the internet now that I had ventured out of the UK.

It was not quite the sort of welcome I was expecting on the Mull of Galloway.

For this wonderfully remote and wild headland, standing at the end of a long and dramatically beautiful road – about 20 miles from the Isle of Man, and only a few miles further from Ireland, both of which you can see on a clear day – is still firmly attached to the mainland of Scotland and is rightly described as one of that country's best kept secrets.

Everywhere you turn there's a stunning view. All around you is the frenzied activity of a huge cliff colony of sea birds, while at your feet the heathland which encompasses the lighthouse is alive with smaller birds, bugs and butterflies.

For anyone interested in wildlife – even if only modestly, like myself – it's a form of paradise. So it was ironic that the first thing I saw when I arrived at the Mull of Galloway was a dog that was so fat that it could not climb out of the back of its owners' car unaided. It had to wait while they unfolded a metal ramp – the sort of thing some shops have to help their disabled customers manage an inconvenient doorstep – which they then propped against the tailgate so the obese mutt could wobble its way to the ground.

The other wildlife on the headland was rather more emotionally uplifting. And I had the benefit of my own personal guided walk, taken by two RSPB wardens who, twice a week, take visitors on a gentle stroll around the Mull, pointing out interesting birds, animals and flowers as they go.

When I saw the notice advertising that such a walk would be leaving the RSPB visitor centre that very afternoon I assumed I would be joining a considerable band of birdwatchers, all dressed in tweed and with impressive binoculars around their necks. But when I arrived at the allotted hour I found just two men – the full-time warden and a volunteer assistant from Yorkshire who was spending a week of his holidays there – and no visitors at all.

They were not in the least perturbed by people's lack of enthusiasm for their walk, or by the relative ignorance of the one person – me – who had bothered to turn up.

"How good are you on birds?" one of them asked.

"Well, I can recognise a gannet," I replied.

"That's more than most people!"

"And I know I'm not allowed just to call everything a seagull. I know there are guillemots and kittiwakes and herring gulls and terns and so on. Just don't ask me which is which."

"That makes you an expert compared with a lot of the people who come here," he said.

Even after the two hours I spent with them exploring the Mull – peering over high cliffs at the birds nesting below, standing as still as statues as we watched the antics of the linnets flitting around the gorse, and watching in silence as the gannets plunged spectacularly into the sea to catch their prey (they not only have reinforced skulls to withstand the thwack as they hit the water, I now know, but also "airbags" inside their heads so that their brains don't get damaged by the impact) – I don't think I'll ever have the patience to make a bird watcher.

It was an interesting afternoon, and though being with my two knowledgeable guides added something to it, they did not make the difference between enjoying it or not. I loved the wildness of the place, the sun, the sea and the gentle wind blowing in my face. But the enjoyment I derived from just being there would have been the same whether or not I could tell the difference between a cormorant and a shag (I still can't).

Back at the visitor centre I turned the conversation towards my Bongo Night adventure – just to find out, without actually asking, whether anyone would object if I spent the night on the car park near the lighthouse. The wardens there were impressed. "That's a great thing to do," said one, who seemed more junior than the rest, but had grasped the point of my conversation better than they. "I bet you've been to some wonderful places. Will you be spending the night here? This would be a great place!"

I pretended that I had not already made up my mind to do so.

"You're right, it would be a great place – but it rather depends on whether I'd be allowed to."

The man I took to be the senior warden pulled the sort of face that could have meant whatever I wanted it to.

"Well, it's not approved of," he said. "And we certainly don't encourage it. But if you did I don't suppose anybody would actually chase you away."

That, I reckoned, was about as close to an invitation as I was going to get.

48
TARN MOOR
Near Penrith, Cumbria
Friday May 29

If I had to choose my favourite location in the Lake District, the one place which gives me a thrill and makes my eyes prickle with its beauty no matter how often I may go there, it would the spot where, after you've been walking for an hour or so over the fells from the little village of Helton, the ground falls away and you find the majesty of Ullswater suddenly spread out before you.

I have said before that Ullswater is my favourite lake, and the sight of it from those fells – so close, yet so wonderfully undiscovered by almost every tourist – never fails to take my breath away.

It would have been an omission, as I neared the end of my Bongo Night adventure, if I had not included a visit there.

Not that you can park a Bongo at that precise point, of course. The spot where the view of Ullswater suddenly unfolds below you is happily distant from anywhere that can be negotiated by anything less robust than a farmer's quadbike. But it is possible to get quite close.

I took the road into Helton, then dived to the right, up a lane that shoots sharply past the last few houses and onto the fellside. Within a mile all sign of civilisation has gone and, were it not for the narrow ribbon of tarmac winding through the gorse, you might think nobody had ever been there before.

They have, of course. It's a favourite place for dog walkers, and for fell walkers who don't mind cheating by using a car to gain them the first thousand feet before they set off on foot to conquer some peak or other. But on that night the only sign of human life was a car parked in a rough lay-by, pointing towards the Pennines to the east, which were already turning gold under the setting sun.

I drove on till I could no longer see it and pulled onto the flattest patch of grass I could find.

Behind me the sun was falling towards the horizon of the moorland, in front of me the Pennines were spread out in a glorious panorama that dimmed even as I watched it, and to my left an extraordinary brown cloud blotted out any hope of a view, a sure sign that Penrith and all the other places I had passed through to get there were now being drenched in a sudden squall.

The only sound I could hear was of the wind gently whistling over the Bongo. The peacefulness, the aloneness, was something to rejoice in. Then three young men, none of whom looked old enough to drive, arrived in a small convoy, and parked their cars side by side, in a neat row not more than 20 feet from me. Their cars – all shining and beautifully polished, with the very latest accessories gleaming in the dying light – were clearly their pride and joy.

They took photographs of them against the setting sun (but only after using their sleeves to wipe off any suggestion of dirt they had picked up on their drive into the hills) and then manoeuvred them a few yards so they could take some more with the sun at a better angle.

In other circumstances – faced with three teenagers on some lonely and increasingly dark hillside – I might have been troubled by a certain apprehension.

But, though I longed for them to go away and leave me to myself, this was the least threatening trio I could have hoped to encounter. Soon enough they drove off as suddenly as they had arrived and I watched in surprise as they took a course not along the road, but over the rough moorland, dodging the bumps and hollows as if they were chasing wildebeest on some overland safari.

I was still trying to work out how they could dish out such treatment to the cars they obviously loved so much when their tail lights disappeared from view behind the undergrowth. I have no idea whether they continued their journey home on some rough track, or doubled back to the road so they could do it on the more welcoming tarmac, but they were gone and that was all that mattered.

I didn't see another soul until I was cooking breakfast the next morning. And by that time I had already been for a walk over the fell to the place where I could enjoy that view, down over Ullswater. It was a perfect morning for it. So perfect that I was already walking by six o'clock. The early sun was shining brightly, the sky was blue and the lake, when it came into view, was a deep purple.

I sat on a rock, with the skylarks singing their beautiful songs just for me.

49
ST ABB'S HEAD
Berwickshire, Scotland
Thursday June 4

When Tricia needed a lift to Edinburgh airport for a girlie day in Brussels with our daughter Juliet, who had been at a conference there, it gave me the opportunity for a Bongo Night well away from my usual haunts.

The east coast of southern Scotland was not a place I would ever normally have considered, but since I had to go to Edinburgh anyway it made sense to make a small diversion and – as I explained to several people I met along the way – take the scenic route home.

I had been to Dunbar before, briefly, and remembered it as an attractive and interesting little place with two distinct harbours – one mostly for fishing boats and one, smaller, more for leisure craft – and I had an idea that one of them would maybe provide a spot for parking overnight.

I arrived there less than two hours after leaving the airport (and that included a lengthy trip through the teeming streets of the capital, on the basis that they were the more interesting option since I knew the city's boring by-pass very well and could not face the prospect of doing it again) and parked for free in the main street while I got my bearings.

I spent some time exploring the place on foot, bought the ingredients for my breakfast from a small Co-op store and quickly decided that my idea of spending the night at the harbour was probably a non-starter. The parking spaces I had visualised myself using – right on the quay, beside the boats – were firmly marked "For Commercial Fishermen Only", and I had no wish to enter into an argument with a burly Scotsman in oilskins and a sou'wester about the rights and wrongs of parking the Bongo there. And the public parking spaces – set slightly away from the harbourside, and therefore less attractive – would still be pretty noisy once the fishermen arrived to go out on the high tide early in the morning.

So I decided that later I would try my luck somewhere else.

Still, Dunbar is a pretty place, the sun was shining and I had plenty of time, so I moved the Bongo to a big car park beside a leisure centre (and, helpfully, public toilets), from where I went on another, longer, walk around the town.

It's funny how some people so clearly want to talk.

This one was a grey-haired, pot-bellied man who was standing on the end of the jetty looking at the boats.

"Making the most of the sunshine?" I asked, sensing that I would get something more than "Yes" for an answer.

"Indeed," he said. And, eyeing the camera I had slung round my neck: "You're a . . . ?"

"Tourist," I said.

"I thought you were a photographer. Though what's the difference between someone who calls himself a photographer and a tourist with a camera? They both do the same thing, but one's more pretentious than the other, I suppose."

He told me he was there on his own, staying in a hotel after putting his wife on a train back to Gloucestershire following a family get-together in Durham. He had already been to Holy Island and the Farne Islands – both nature reserves off the Northumbria coast further south – and was looking forward to a boat trip to Bass Rock – the huge volcanic lump that dominates the seascape for miles around and which is famously home to 150,000 nesting gannets – the next day.

"You're into birds then," I commented, rather unnecessarily, I thought.

"No, not really."

We continued our walks in opposite directions – he back to his hotel and I onto the breakwater for a quick look at the nesting kittiwakes on the cliff – and as I returned to the car park along the other side of the harbour I made way for a 4x4 driven by a woman with, presumably, her teenaged daughter in the passenger seat.

She stopped and made no attempt to pass me, even though I had made plenty of space. Then I noticed that both she and her daughter were staring into the harbour. I followed their gaze and saw they were looking at a seal basking lazily between the fishing boats.

"Thank you," I told her through her open window. "I wouldn't have spotted it if you hadn't been here."

"He's always here, that one," she said. "Every day. He knows when he's well off. The fishermen feed him. They're asking for trouble if you ask me."

She was obviously local, so I asked her if she knew anywhere where I could safely spend the night in the Bongo. She suggested a place just a mile north, Belhaven Bay, where there was a big car park facing a huge sandy bay, which was a favourite with both campervanners and people taking photographs of the sunset over the sea.

"That sounds ideal," I said, and thanked her.

Belhaven Bay was not what she had led me to expect. There was indeed a glorious bay, and a huge car park, but it was sandwiched between two enormous caravan sites, and dotted with signs proclaiming "No Overnight Parking".

I stayed just long enough to scoff the fish and chips I'd just bought at the town's award-winning chipshop, admired the local tourist attraction (the "bridge to nowhere" – a construction that appears to lead to nothing more exciting than a different part of the beach) and decided it was time to head south to a wilder part of the country where, I hoped, I would be allowed to sleep undisturbed.

A couple of wild goose chases later – one of which would have presented me with an ideal place to park the Bongo had it not been for the fact that it was on the private land of one of Scotland's foremost organic vegetable growers – and I was in one of the best of all my Bongo Night locations.

A fine modern signpost pointed the way to "Dowlaw 2 miles", and made no mention of the fact that it was a no through road, even though that's what it turned out to be. It led over increasingly wild moorland, with tantalising glimpses of the sea far below and numerous potential Bongo spots along the way. Eventually a hand-painted sign near a cattle grid announced "Dowlaw Farm" and there was no doubt that, though spoiled for choice as far as camping places were concerned, I was now on private land.

My problem was simple: Should I simply park there, among the wandering sheep on the grass just inside the cattle grid, and pretend that I had not noticed the farm sign (a difficult thing to do, since it stood imperiously just behind me), or should I accept that I could not park on private land and go and find somewhere else?

The trouble was, it was such a perfect area for wildcamping I was loathe to give it up.

It was, I also discovered, in an area with a remarkably strong mobile phone signal – important for what I had planned for the next morning.

So I drove on for half a mile or so – far enough away from the farm sign to at least add some little credence to any claim that I had not seen it – then pulled onto the grass and manoeuvred the Bongo so that it was on an almost level piece of land and looking at the sea.

I was facing north-west, looking towards the imposing cliffs around North Berwick, with the great dark mass of Bass Rock slowly disappearing as the sky and sea turned into a breathtaking array of purples and oranges as the sun set around it.

It was the most spectacular display of all the sunsets I had witnessed on my Bongo travels.

Nobody came to tell me that I should not have parked there. Indeed, apart from a young man in a van delivering something to the farm which I guessed must be at the end of the road, I did not see another human in all the hours I was there.

I woke to the bright sunshine of dawn, early enough to go for a walk along the clifftop before returning to the Bongo to use my mobile to log onto the internet to listen to my son Will's band, which at seven o'clock that morning was playing live on the bandstand in Carlisle as part of the BBC's first Music Day, in which mostly unheard-of musicians were being given the chance of a day in the national spotlight.

Hearing his band mylittlebrother playing live at such an early hour was surreal enough, but hearing it while sitting on a cliff overlooking the Bass Rock made it even more so.

With most Bongo Nights I am happy to cut the umbilical cord which links me with home; on this occasion I was glad that the miracles of modern communications had made it possible for me to join in such an occasion, even at 100 miles arm's length.

A few miles south of my night-time campsite lay St Abb's Head, a craggy promontory and nature reserve famous for its spectacular views and the clamouring calls of thousands of sea birds. When I pulled into the car park at 8am I was the first vehicle there, so it looked for all the world as if I had spent the night there. I took delight in positioning the Bongo next to a sign that warned "Strictly no camping or overnight parking" and found myself almost hoping that later on some bolshie National Trust for Scotland warden would falsely accuse me of disobeying the rules. The only way I could prove I had not, I knew, would be to show him my camera with its photographs of the previous night's sunset taken from up on the cliff overlooking Bass Rock.

I took a four-mile walk around the headland, past the lighthouse (the only one in Britain where you have to climb down to get to it, apparently – if they had built it, as normal, on top of the cliffs it would too often have been obliterated by the fog for which the place is notorious) and back to the car park, all by ten o'clock.

Along the way I saw not a soul, apart from a young couple who had been given the job of studying the rocks with a high-powered pair of binoculars, and counting the number of eggs in the kittiwake nests.

Back at the car park I was pleased to see that a National Trust Land-Rover was now parked beside the Bongo, but disappointed to find that nobody emerged from it to tell me off for spending the night there.

50
KERSHOPE
England-Scotland border
Friday June 12

In 48 years of driving I had never been booked for speeding. But that was probably because in the 50 years I had been supporting Bristol City I had never known a season like it.

The club I had supported for so long – a club more associated with words such as failure, disappointment and defeat – had suddenly become synonymous with success, excitement and victory.

From the opening day of the season (when we defeated promotion favourites Sheffield United on Bongo Night No 6), right through the dark cold days of winter and into the bright promise of spring (Bongo Night No 40), City had been at the very top of the league table for all but a few days. We had defeated almost everyone we had played – usually with some style – and those of us who over the years had been browbeaten into expecting defeat, were now, joyously, disappointed by anything less than a win.

And so it was that I travelled to Bradford City for one of our last games of the season, knowing that a victory would secure the promotion that had by now become almost, but not quite certain.

A 1-0 win would have done, though I knew that would be difficult because Bradford City were on something of a winning streak themselves, and anyway gaining the last few points to achieve promotion was notoriously difficult for even the best of teams (even good players tend to freeze and find themselves unable to give their best when so much is at stake).

I went there – a distance of some 112 miles from home – not in expectation, but, in true Bristol City mood, in a faint hope of sneaking the victory that would finally make the prize ours.

We won 6-0 and it could have been more. Never had I seen a Bristol City team so imperiously brush aside any opponent. Our attacking play was relentless, our players demonstrating skills which I had not dared hope they possessed, and by the end – with the City fans chanting "Oooh aah it's a massacre" and even the Bradford supporters rising to applaud our supremacy – I could barely believe what I had witnessed.

No wonder that on the way home, at Kirkby Lonsdale – driving not the Bongo, but my wife's high-powered Subaru – I was on such a high that I missed both the speed limit sign and the camera that followed.

Because I had no previous convictions I was allowed to opt for a Speed Awareness Course rather than submit to penalty points on my licence, so on Friday June 12 I presented myself at a Carlisle hotel for a morning at which I and 24 other miscreants would have the error of our speeding ways pointed out to us.

It was, in fact, surprisingly interesting, and I don't mind admitting I came out, I like to think, a better driver than I went in.

But I was left with the feeling that the Bongo Night I had pencilled in for that night should, if possible, involve an appropriate speeding theme.

A quick look on the internet gave me what I wanted: A car rally was being held next day in the Scottish Borders, and – even better – it was very close to one of the potential parking places that for many months I'd had at the back of my mind without ever getting round to actually using. And so it was that for Bongo Night No 50 I headed for the Kershope Forest, which straddles the English-Scottish border not 20 miles away from home.

My chosen spot – within walking distance of what I thought would probably be one of the wildest stages of the rally – was in a small quarry, just on the Scottish side of the river which forms the national boundary. Behind me were the rugged moors leading deep into Scotland, while in front of me, and to my left and right, were mile upon mile of trees through which next day the cars would be hurtling.

I was not in the least surprised when, just as I was eating my supper, an old VW campervan pulled in and parked beside me. It was such an obvious places for rally fans to spend the night, so as to be up bright and early for the next day's adventures, that I was surprised there weren't more.

When I'd finished my meal – and seen that the sole occupant of the other van had finished his too – I got out to say hello.

This was Huddersfield Mick, a man who had been following rallying for more than 50 years and who, having taken early retirement, was using the old van his late parents had bequeathed him to travel all over the country to indulge his passion.

In most circumstances I would have cursed him for disturbing the peace of my parking place, but here – on the eve of a sporting event of which I was totally ignorant – I was delighted to see him, and told him so.

"I've never been to a car rally before so I don't know where to go or what to do," I told him, "so I'm afraid you're going to have to tell me."

He was, I'm happy to say, not a man who needed a second invitation to pass on to a novice all the knowledge that half a century of rally-watching had given him, and he imparted it in the sort of thick Yorkshire accent that, in a TV programme, might have been dismissed as laughably exaggerated.

I learned about engines, handbrakes and the different ways of cheating by adding stuff to your petrol even though it was officially banned. I learned about crash helmets, triple anchor seat belts and the special horn that in a rally car has to be near the handbrake so it can be operated by either the driver or the navigator to call for help in an emergency. And I learned that the best drivers go first, and that by the time the novices get a go the course has been so badly chewed up by so much harsh braking and accelerating that they'll find it hard just to keep their cars on the road.

Mick was a fine and enthusiastic teacher and there seemed almost nothing about rallying that he did not know. One thing he did not know, though, was where the hell the next day's rally was being held.

Both of us knew it was somewhere in that area, but in that quiet and remote valley there was nothing to suggest precisely where it might be.

He – like I – had been expecting to arrive at the parking place to find arrows directing us to the next day's car parks from where the action would be seen, or maybe red and white tape to prevent spectators getting too close to danger.

But there was nothing.

"'Spect we'll find out in t'morning," he said.

With that a white car pulled up, whose driver asked us if we knew where the spectators' car park was.

A black van arrived too, and the driver assured us that the best viewing area would be up the track to our left, but I ignored everything he told us after he insisted with the help of the map on his knee that he had come from the north even though we had very definitely just seen him coming down the hill from the south.

If I understood the ensuing conversation correctly (and, since it was conducted in three different, but equally impenetrable accents, none of which seemed to have much in common with English, I'm not sure that I did) nobody knew quite where the rally was being held because the man whose job it had been to update the relevant website had been taken to hospital, and indeed died, before he had had the chance to include a map.

"We'll find out in t'morning when all t'others come," said Mick. "There'll be loads of 'em. By six o'clock, I reckon. Then all we'll have to do is follow them."

I had confidence in Mick. In his quiet way he exuded a kind of knowledgeable calmness, a feeling that everything would become clear if we just had the patience to allow it all to unfold in its own good time.

"I hope you won't mind if I just attach myself to you," I told him when the others had gone.

"I'm one of twins," he laughed, "so all my life I've had someone else following me around. I'm well used to it. You'll be welcome. It won't bother me at all."

It was still early, and a nice evening, so we decided to go for a walk to explore the track which the van driver had assured us led to the viewing area.

"I reckon we're on the course," said Mick, as we rounded a bend to be confronted by a line of red and white tape. "We won't be able to come here tomorrow because there'll be cars coming along here at 80 miles an hour."

"Not the best way to the viewing area, then?"

"Nope."

I liked Mick, though the only thing we had in common was that we had both happened to park our campervans in the same small car park.

He told me he had grown up in Huddersfield, where his mother was "in service" and his father worked in a steelworks. He left school on the day his headmaster labelled him as "unemployable", and went on to work in a variety of jobs – most of them outdoors – until, after his parents' deaths, he inherited enough money to retire at the age of 55.

As we returned to the car park he pointed to the VW van that his father had bought new nearly 20 years before.

"I don't need much else," he said.

He opened the side door and stepped back from the heat.

"Bloody 'ell," he said.

All the time we had been out walking a kettle had been boiling over a low heat on the gas hob. It had now boiled dry and was giving off the unmistakable smell of red hot metal.

"Bloody 'ell," he said again. "Just as well we came back."

Mick grabbed the kettle with a cloth and threw it on the ground, where it sizzled on the damp gravel.

"That could have been awkward. Do you want a beer?"

We spent the rest of the evening leaning on his van, drinking Budweiser (not my favourite beer) and cursing the midges which the citronella candle I had fetched from the Bongo was doing little to deter.

The next morning proved I was right to have faith in Mick. At six o'clock we – and the two other vans and three cars which had arrived during the night – were joined by "all t'others" as he had forecast. A variety of cars and trucks came down the hill behind us and drove up the track which we had walked up the night before.

By now the area was festooned with all the arrows and signs we had been expecting from the start – including a "No entry for spectators" sign on our lane, and an arrow to "Car park" pointing up the hill in England, on the far side of the river.

The place was filling up with rally fans, some of whom actually knew what was going on.

After talking to one of them Mick reported that we were more handily placed than we thought. While we could not walk along the track by the river because it was part of the course, all we had to do was go a little way up the hill, then about a mile down another track and we would find ourselves in the thick of the area set aside for spectators.

The only question was whether we should drive our vans there or walk.

"It'll be a narrow track with nowhere to turn and when it's all over it'll take ages to get out . . . so let's walk," he said.

It took an hour to get there – a pleasant enough walk through the trees – and Mick spent every minute explaining to me the significance of some of what I was about to see. The way Car 000 goes around first, opening the course and checking that all the "street furniture" is in place, then Car 00 does the same to check that there are no spectators in dangerous places, and then Car 0 (a rally car driven by someone specially invited for the job) goes around at high speed. Once that car has completed the course, and the driver reported that there are no problems, we are all set for action.

The action, when it came, was quite exciting.

The sight of a car hurtling along a bumpy gravel track at speeds which in other circumstances would have landed him in court, skidding around bends and slithering alarmingly close to ditches and tree stumps is indeed just as thrilling as Mick had promised me it would be.

The sight of a second car doing the same is also pretty thrilling . . .

And a third, fourth and even fifth . . .

But 138 of them? For me the excitement had passed, and been replaced by something approaching boredom, long before the end, and I ended the morning sitting on a log in the sunshine, hardly even bothering to watch.

Only when one car, travelling noticeably more slowly than those at the front of the field, gently drifted off the track and got stuck in the ditch right in front of me was my interest rekindled.

"Did you see 'im?" Mick asked. "He was driving like he was on a Sunday afternoon out. He was driving like some old man just out for a jolly. I bet he's got his picnic hamper in the boot."

I was surprised by that, remembering that Mick had told me that those at the back of the pack were probably "young lads" just beginning their rallying careers, but again he was proved right.

As the driver clambered from his stricken car – so firmly wedged in the ditch that the combined muscles of half a dozen spectators couldn't shift it – we could see from his ample belly that this was no lithe teenager.

He took off his crash helmet to reveal the thinning white hair of a man of about my age.

Indeed, in a dim light he might have looked rather like me.

"Ha! That reminds me how you came to be here," Mick laughed. "You thought it would be fun to see a load of people driving very very fast with no danger of being caught by a speed camera. So was it worth it?"

"Oh yes," I told him. "It's been a lot of fun."

"And will you be back?"

"Probably not."

51
CONISTON
Cumbria
Monday June 15

My response to anyone asking why I was doing all this has always been "If you have to ask I can't be bothered to tell you" – a perhaps unnecessarily curt way of explaining that if you can't recognise the sheer freedom and delight of exploring the country in an ancient campervan there is nothing I can do to explain it.

Even so, it was only when I was well into my year – even as late as the 51st of my 52 Bongo Nights – that I came to realise that what I was doing was, in many people's eyes, quite special.

The number of people who had 'liked' my regular posts to the Bongo owners' group on Facebook had been steadily increasing, as had their admiring comments – anything ranging from "This is just such a fantastic challenge" and "Wow, what a brilliant idea" to "Blinkin' marvellous" and "You're such a dude!" had become commonplace.

And people I met along the way, to whom I explained that I was planning to park in some god forsaken lay-by in some remote place with only sheep for company, seemed to be becoming increasingly impressed by it all.

The best example of this was after Bongo Night No 51, the only one I had planned several months in advance.

I had enjoyed watercolour painting for years, ever since my daughter Juliet gave me a portable set – a small blue carrying case containing paints, sketchbook, pencil, pencil sharpener, rubber, brushes and water bottle – in the hope that it would give me something to do on the many occasions when I went on a country walk with Tricia only to find myself at a loose end while she got out her binoculars and watched birds for what seemed like hours on end.

My artistic endeavours have been mixed – many have been rubbish, but a few, I'm not too modest to say, have been surprisingly good – but I had always wondered how much better they might be with a lesson or two.

So in October last year I Googled "watercolour lessons in Cumbria" and booked myself onto a course run by a lady called Jackie Hadwin at her studio near Coniston in the Lake District.

She had no vacancies until June, but that suited me fine because, even though I did not know that area very well, I was confident there would be several fine overnight parking spots near Coniston, so it would give me the opportunity of combining my painting lesson with my last-but-one Bongo Night.

On the fells above Coniston, at the end of a gated road that leads to Walna Scar, there is a rough-hewn car park much used by fell walkers and climbers as they set off for some strenuous excitement on the mountain known as the Old Man which towers above it.

It was the perfect spot for my penultimate Bongo Night – a peaceful hideaway with fantastic views in every direction, remote yet within a couple of miles of a village and (importantly for this occasion) just a 15 minute drive from Jackie's studio.

When I arrived early in the evening, after a sublime drive through some of the loveliest parts of the Lake District, there were just a few other cars there, all waiting for their owners to return from whatever physical challenges they had been involved with higher up. A minibus from Newton Rigg College, near Penrith, was disgorging about a dozen students who were all laughter and jollity as they set off across the fells, under the weight of some surprisingly large rucsacs, for a night camping under the stars.

Gradually the owners of the cars returned, none giving me a second glance, and soon I had the place to myself – or I did, anyway, if you discount the sheep, the lonely mallard swimming on the enormous puddle (or small lake, it was difficult to tell) by which I parked the van, and the single remaining car parked slightly lower down the hill.

Sometime in the evening a shiny black 4x4 turned up, in which a young man endeavoured to impress his girlfriend by driving it up one of the 45 degree rocky inclines in a small quarry just behind the Bongo . . . until it got stuck and he had to get out to give it a crestfallen shove backwards.

Another car – a small thing like a Nissan Micra – came up the hill and disappeared along a track which seemed to lead to absolutely nowhere.

And just before sunset a man and his very small son – surely no more than four years old, but wearing good strong boots and wielding two walking poles – came off the fell and made for the one last car. I could not decide whether to applaud the father for instilling a love of the outdoors into such a small child or to condemn him for exposing him to what must have been some danger so late in the day.

After that . . . almost total silence. With the sound of the sheep baaing gently in the distance, and the occasional quack from my duck on the puddle, I really did have the place to myself.

I still had it to myself the next morning and was eating my breakfast by the time I saw my first human – a frail-looking elderly lady who belied her appearance by striding across the fell with her two labradors after arriving in her Ford Focus.

It was such a spectacularly beautiful location I was loathe to leave it, but my plan was to drive down to Coniston (public toilets assume an almost unhealthy attraction after a night wild camping) before heading on to Jackie and my painting lesson.

I arrived in the village almost before it had woken up, went for a walk, used the lavatory in the boatyard . . . and still had time to spend an hour playing my guitar while parked beside the lake.

Jackie Hadwin's studio was an extraordinarily beautiful building (to call it a barn conversion would not be doing it justice) tucked against the rising moorland in the village of Torver. There were six of us 'students' – me, two women from Kendal, one from Windermere and two elderly ladies from Canada – all of us proclaiming a lack of artistic ability (a claim which for all of us probably owed more to modesty than reality, judging from our results as the day progressed).

Jackie turned out to be not just a very talented artist – her paintings hanging on the studio wall served as both incentive and intimidation – but a remarkably patient and gentle tutor. She was also a very good cook and it was over lunch – an excellent vegetable lasagne followed by Eton Mess or pie made from the rhubarb out of her garden – that the conversation turned to what we were all doing there.

One of the Kendal ladies had been given the course as a birthday present, and her friend had liked the sound of it and come along as well; the Windermere woman had bought the lesson for herself because she had always been too frightened to try her hand at painting without having some know-how to get her started; and the two Canadians were on a six-week tour of Europe, and had found Jackie's website because they had a particular interest in art.

"And I'm here because 51 weeks ago I decided to see if I could spend a night in my campervan every week for a whole year," I told them.

The response was extraordinary.

It was as if I'd told them that I'd once been one of the Beatles (a couple of them had spotted my guitar on the Bongo's passenger seat) or maybe that I'd won the Nobel Prize for Nuclear Science, or set the world speed record by swimming the length of Coniston Water before breakfast.

The mouths of the two Canadian ladies literally dropped open.

"That's wonderful, that's incredible, that's so brave, that's such a fantastic thing to do."

Their excitement and the awe in which they now held me was somehow unsettling.

"It's a pretty pointless thing to have done, to be honest," I said, trying to diffuse some of the undeserved admiration.

"No, not pointless at all," they insisted. "It's wonderful, it's incredible, it's so brave, it's a fantastic thing to do . . ."

The three Cumbrian ladies, though not quite so over-the-top in their enthusiasm, made it plain that they believed it was quite special too. "Good for you," one of them said.

That night I returned home, posted my latest photographs on the Facebook Bongo pages and almost immediately got more than 100 'likes'.

OK, I thought to myself at last, maybe my Bongo Night challenge was a bit more exciting than I thought.

52
ULLSWATER
Cumbria
Saturday June 27

I was approaching my 52nd and final Bongo Night with mixed feelings. I had enjoyed the other 51 more than I had ever have expected and though I knew I would enjoy the satisfaction of completing the task there was a part of me that dreaded it coming to an end.

Despite the rain and the cold, the wind and the snow – and the injured back and the broken leg – what had started as a vague idea hatched as a way of giving me something to do in my retirement had become an almost all consuming passion which had added a new dimension to my life.

And the further I got into it – and the more people I told about it – the more had my determination to complete the challenge increased.

Yes, there had been times – particularly in the middle of winter – when I wished I didn't have to set off into yet another night in the dark and the rain with nothing but a guitar, a book and a crackling radio for company.

But those times were far outnumbered by those on which my heart sang when I pulled back the curtains and saw the latest wild and beautiful place which, for just a few wonderful hours, I had entirely to myself.

I knew that I had to do something very special to mark the conclusion of this marvellous, exciting, unforgettable adventure.

After a year like that I could not just go and park in some lonely lay-by, wake up, admire the view . . . and head home.

It needed something exceptional..

And (as no one who has got this far in this account of my Bongo Challenge will be surprised to hear) it just had to be at Ullswater which, as I've said several times before and I shall now say for the last time, is my favourite of all the Lake District lakes.

So I hired a boat.

And 52 weeks after Tricia and I spent that night on that small caravan park overlooking the Duddon estuary, we and 52 friends and relatives had a big party.

(It is entirely coincidental – and, indeed I have only just realised it, writing this several weeks after the event – that there, helping us celebrate my 52-week Bongo Night challenge on that cruise around lovely Ullswater, was precisely one friend for each Bongo Night.)

The Lady of the Lake is a magnificent green-hulled, red funnelled boat, which, at nearly 140 years old, is reckoned to be the oldest working passenger vessel in the world.

She was built at Rutherglen near Glasgow in 1877, and then had to be transported in three sections by rail to Penrith, from where she was dragged – still in three pieces – by horse and cart to Pooley Bridge, on the shores of Ullswater, where she was assembled.

We hired her for the evening, and spent two hours cruising in the (mostly) sun, rejoicing in being among some of the finest scenery Britain – and indeed the world – has to offer, and afterwards those of us lucky enough to have campervans of our own spent the night parked beside that gorgeous lake, in the car park beside the jetty.

Two Bongos (one of my daughter Jules's friends came in a very smart, bright blue one) and nine other campervans, all gathered there at the waterside to help me celebrate the successful conclusion of my crazy, tremendous, brilliant Bongo Night challenge. It was, I confess, a tear-jerking end to what had often been a tear-jerking year.

I look back on some of those times – sitting on a rock at Malin Head, just playing my guitar and singing to the stars; hearing the spine-tingling call of the stags at their early morning rut in the Lake District; watching the spectacular sunset, and a few hours later the indescribable sunrise, from my piece of lonely moorland near Hay-on-Wye . . .

I think back of the people I met along the way – the young Lebanese musicians in the pub in Keswick, the drunken woman who pointed me to an idyllic wildcamping spot in the Yorkshire Dales, and the friendly monk who took pity on us in the rain at his temple in the Scottish Borders . . .

And I thank with all my heart the people who have followed my adventures – and who, like Tricia and the rest of my family – have given me endless encouragement through the good times and the bad.

Crazy idea, maybe it was.

But it was one of the most extraordinary years of my life.

And if you have to ask me why I did it . . . I can't be bothered to tell you.

THE END

ABOUT THE AUTHOR

Richard Harris is a retired journalist and
one-time evening newspaper editor
who spent more than 40 years
in the UK provincial newspaper industry.
He grew up in Somerset and began his career
in Weston-super-Mare. He went on to work
on newspapers in Bristol and Nottingham before
moving to Carlisle more than 25 years ago.
He now lives in a small village in North Cumbria.